inHER
POWER
inHER
WiSDOM

A WOMAN'S GUIDE TO
Overcoming Challenges and
Growing Into Your Power

You are powerful!

Rebecca Now

COMPILED BY
Rebecca Now &
Dr. Marty K. Casey

InHer Power InHer Wisdom
A Woman's Guide to Overcoming Challenges and Growing Into Your Power
Herstory Press

Published by **Herstory Press**, St. Louis, MO
Copyright ©2024

Cover, Interior Design, and Project Management:
  Davis Creative Publishing, DavisCreativePublishing.com

Writing Coach and Editor: Marie Chewe-Elliott

Compilation by Rebecca Now and Dr. Marty K. Casey

Library of Congress Cataloging-in-Publication Data

Library of Congress Control Number: 2024912625

InHer Power InHer Wisdom: A Woman's Guide to Overcoming Challenges and Growing Into Your Power

ISBN: 979-8-9873049-4-5 (paperback)
      979-8-9873049-1-4 (ebook)
1. SEL021000   SELF-HELP / Motivational & Inspirational   2. SEL031000
      SELF-HELP / Personal Growth / General   3. OCC019000 BODY, MIND &
      SPIRIT / Inspiration & Personal Growth
2024

Dedication
Our book is dedicated to
all of our daughters,
Rebecca's daughter, Molly
and Marty's daughter, Morgan,
as well as all daughters worldwide.
May all of our daughters step into their power
and experience political and
cultural equality as well as respect.

Table of Contents

Maxine Clark

Foreword

When the Delmar Divine opened its doors in 2022, it created a space, a physical space for people to connect and find solutions to the deep disparities in our region. St. Louis, like many cities in the country, is plagued by a divide of rich and poor, many times along sharp racial lines. The fragmentation of our communities has been an impediment to finding solutions to problems.

This book creates a space for women to come together and share their stories, to be vulnerable about challenging moments in their lives, and to reflect and realize how they overcame their personal life events and move forward.

In the book, you will experience stories of tragic loss of loved ones, overcoming a less-than-ideal upbringing, surviving being bullied and shunned and many more stories that create a connection to our rich tapestry of human experiences. Each story in this book contains pearls of wisdom, forged in a difficult time in each woman's life.

Women have historically been held back from fully participating in all aspects of our society, and the record of women of differing races has been fraught with a separatism, distrust and racism. That was then, and this is now. When you handle and resolve difficult situations in life you gain powerful life experience that can be used to help others realize their value as well. We do not have to have the same life experiences to learn from others—quite the contrary. We need to go forward together. And it starts with sharing our stories and developing personal connections.

There are no easy solutions to our problems, whether it is gun violence, domestic abuse, or disparities in the quality of education, food, or health care. And no one person can solve them all. It takes working together: black and white, young and old, men and women.

I personally know the two authors that compiled this book, and both Dr. Marty K. Casey and Rebecca Now are both incredibly giving people who are engaged in our community. Our mutual friend, Karen Hoffman put the two of them together, demonstrating that it takes just one person to make a powerful connection.

My philosophy is 1 + 1 = 1000. In today's world there is a multiplier effect in a single collaboration. Marty and Rebecca have come together to create a vibrant community of authors in this book, and you, the reader, have expanded that circle. It is time to work together and heal St. Louis, the nation, and the world.

Happy Reading!
Maxine Clark
CEO, Clark-Fox Family Foundation
Founder, Build-A-Bear Workshop
Chief INspirator, The Delmar DivINe

Dr. Marty K. Casey

Born in Purpose

"Find out who you are and do it on purpose."
— Dolly Parton

Thinking back, as a little girl, playing alone in my bedroom with my Barbie dolls, if anyone had witnessed my creative play, they would have been alarmed to discover that something was deeply hurting inside me, causing a great deal of emotional pain. See, I never played with my dolls lovingly. They were always in some sort of conflict or argument. In my mind, my male doll, Ken, and my female doll, Barbie, didn't love each other. I never played with them in getting along; the sad part was that I pulled these emotions from a real place. I was witnessing domestic violence in my home.

This caused fear to stick in my subconscious. However, through creative play, I was mentally able to practice solving problems of violence quickly—just like I do today with clients in my company, UnGUN Institute. This type of play stimulated me and temporarily numbed feelings of my emotional pain while pushing my brain into high critical, creative thinking mode to keep me safe! This is how the arts saved my life.

At eight years old, playing for hours in my closet with no lights, three shelves, and just the sound of my voice, I controlled the relationship between the dolls. I often ensured that Barbie would beat Ken up after he started the argument, of course. She would smack him, knocking him to the floor, and then quickly rush out of the house (my closet) to catch her Barbie airplane with her little sister Skipper. They would laugh and celebrate their escape from Ken's verbal and physical abuse by flying all over the world (my room). As a little girl, playing alone felt safe and freeing. Looking back on it, I realize how ironic it was to have my dolls argue in the dark inside an isolated place with no witnesses and then begin to pretend to have fun out in the open space of my room. I wonder how many women today live life like that? How many of you are being "closet abused" like my mother and Barbie? They both, on the outside, appeared to have the perfect life. But in actuality, they were both broken in so many ways.

My mother's choice to stay with her alcoholic husband for so long pushed me into becoming the recipient of suppressed anger for years.

Trying to cope with the feelings I didn't understand, I created and acted out what I wanted to see in my mind. As an adult, I later became a professional actress.

Most of my roles have been mothers with extreme emotional trauma experiences. No surprises here.

My mother later admitted that she only stayed in the marriage because she didn't want to hurt my brother and me with a divorce. However, it was what we witnessed in the broken marriage that scarred us for life. By the time she finally gained the strength to leave, it was too late. The unthinkable happened.

All grown up, who is this actress, singer, and activist from the north side of St. Louis, Lee and Shreve Avenues, to be exact? She's the woman who decided to heal the little girl inside of her and become a global peace ambassador!

Although it was years before I would find my voice from all the trauma, I remember that it was in the stillness that I could find my inner peace. There, I discovered the most comforting place for me, on stage, where I could release my gifts through performance and speaking engagements. This is where I could help others through the power of arts, and I discovered my power isn't me making a fist and swinging it; it's me making a fist to hold a mic in it! Change didn't happen overnight. It only took me several fights, a few suspensions, and almost being locked up a couple of times to get the big picture! However, after I chose to change, I did. I chose my singing ability over my anger every time. Anger can cause us to lose so much, and I was losing my way until I found my purpose.

Many people struggle to find purpose. They search, hoping to stumble across something that marks them worthy and pushes them into doing extraordinary things with their gifts and talents. I wish I could simultaneously send a message to all eight billion people, "Just look inside yourself!" Hurt people, hurt people. Healed people, heal people. Most people hurting operate from a place of pain. We must choose to move from violence to value. When you value yourself, you begin to value others. Remember, self-worth automatically increases when you operate in your purpose. This increases inner love for self, decreasing outer harm towards others. You were born with your purpose. You don't become it! You walk in it!

You might be going through something at this very moment, and it's extremely taxing and emotionally draining. I get it! Watching my mother struggle to raise my brother and me after the divorce was hard. She stopped the domestic violence but entered into a financial struggle. We faced several evictions because of it.

This caused my brother to turn to the streets, and it made me turn to men who could buy me nicer things. In my freshman year of college, I got pregnant with a beautiful baby girl, forcing me to drop out. With no savings, bad credit, or a full-time job, I inherited some of those same financial hardships, like my mother. This pushed me to rely on government assistance, including food stamps. The trauma of it all made me realize that I had completely lost control of my self-worth. I find it rewarding today to give back specifically to young ladies. I will never judge them because I will always remember that I was them once.

Solutions are hard to discover when the problems are wrapped up in uncontrollable amounts of hurt and pain! We start to question our destiny. We wonder if we have what it takes to push through. Yes, we do! Because it's only a moment of emotional distress, and this too shall pass. Don't give up!!!

I promise the answers and the next steps will appear. You just have to be still to hear your inner "mind, body, and spirit" speaking to you. My great-grandmother, Nanny, was among the wisest women I ever knew. She often said, "There's nothing new under the sun." Trust me when I tell you she was right; everything you're experiencing is for a reason, and it will match up with something you have already encountered. Our lives are like a 5000-piece puzzle. Each experience fits perfectly together, and no two pieces are alike. You must trust the process and know that every part will fit perfectly, even when it feels imperfect and impossible.

The most traumatic time of my life was when my parents separated before their divorce. During this time, my father's grandmother was shot and killed in her home on Good Friday by two men who broke in only to steal a black and white TV. Later that same summer, one afternoon, I found my mother lying face down in our restroom, gasping for breath because she had taken a handful of prescription pills trying to end her life. I don't think I will ever get the image of the bottle and pills lying around her lifeless-looking body. Still, to this day, I have a hard time taking prescription pills for myself. This is the result of my being triggered. At the time, I recall quickly dialing 911 and three large male paramedics pumping my mother's little stomach on our tiny restroom floor before wheeling her out of the house on a gurney. I got my mother the help she needed in time, and I finally got her to see it was time to FIGHT BACK! She said that seeing her little girl see her as weak was an even more significant pain for her to overcome. It took months; however, after talking to a psychiatrist and gaining her strength back, my mother never attempted to retake her life. Her doctor helped her to see that hurting herself wasn't going to stop those who had hurt her. The only way to stop them would be to remove them from her life by loving them from a distance.

This is when I learned that taking time to build ourselves up is necessary and healthy to stay emotionally safe. How do we learn self-care or self-love? If these practices were taught in schools K-12, how many young girls' lives could we impact? I believe that when girls know their value, they are less likely to be subjected to domestic violence. My understanding now of what my mother was experiencing teaches me to practice my self-worth and maintain a healthy level of confidence. Tapping into these areas allows me to understand that no one controls my emotions. I am responsible for my feelings and must process them and respond accordingly. Knowing the difference between the energy we exchange and the feelings and emotions we experience is essential. Trauma and healing are transferable; however, they are both energy fields. We must be intentional about who we engage with and what energy we produce because this can affect us. We can never change what happens to us. We can only change how we feel about it. Trauma has no face, place, or race. Trauma doesn't discriminate. It's important to keep yourself emotionally balanced to limit some of the emotional triggers in and around you. I learned that I would quickly react to protect myself out of fear. This reaction caused more harm.

After discovering that self-control could keep me safer than physically fighting, I gained much more value in relationships and opportunities.

Learning this late in life almost cost me my education. By the time I was in 9th grade, I had already attended ten different schools, and it was at the second high school that I graduated from that I discovered I could practice self-care, self-control, and self-love. I'm proud to say that today, I'm the first African-American woman inducted into the Wall of Fame for the class of 1989 at Webster Groves High School. This was one of my greatest accomplishments in life. I can honestly say this was a full-circle moment. Violence produces trauma, trauma, seeks healing, and healing uncovers peace.

When we allow ourselves to heal, we grow and operate from our greatest purpose! I did one simple thing to achieve this life-changing experience: I learned to stop, breathe, and think! Practicing this simple peace response has helped me tremendously!

I have created curricula and workshops, purchased billboards, and held speaking engagements to encourage others to do the same. They taught us to stop, drop, and roll in school if we ever caught on fire. No one ever taught us what to do when it feels like your brain is on fire! When we know better, we can do better and live better! If you're in a time of emotional crisis, Stop! Breathe. Think!

Healing is not a one-time decision. It is a lifetime change that can transform you from broken pieces to living in PEACE!

Dr. Marty K. Casey, a Global Peace Ambassador, has built a fulfilling and impactful career that traverses entertainment and community service as an anointed singer, gifted actress, writer, producer, and director. No matter what hat she wears, her noteworthy goal is "to heal our community, to provide a response and outlet for inbred trauma."

Dr. Casey supports individuals, families, and communities to heal with her latest development of UnGUN Institute©, focused on disarming trauma in individuals and addressing collective trauma events that plague the Black communities.

In 2020, just days before a global pandemic forced a lockdown, Dr. Marty performed her one-woman show in the Big Apple for the most prominent non-profit nationwide, AARP Brooklyn, New York.

Featured on the "St. Louis Business Journal" cover, Dr. Marty is revered as one of the Top 25 Most Influential Businesswomen in St. Louis. In 2021 and 2023, she received the Presidential Lifetime Achievement Award signed by President Joseph R. Biden.

Globally recognized as a transformational trauma coach, Dr. Marty K. Casey remains committed to equipping as many people as possible with strategies, tools, and techniques such as STOP! Breathe. Think!

Please scan this QR code to connect with the author.

Rebecca Now

Thailand Trauma and
a Journey of Self-Discovery

Finishing my bachelor's degree was only a dream when, in my mid-60s, I had the good fortune to continue my studies that I had abandoned 44 years ago. The achievement of a degree was now within reach despite coming late in life. I was on the path to graduation when the discovery of a study-abroad trip to Thailand lured me with pictures of elephants and palm trees. I thought the trip would be the adventure of a lifetime, but it became a traumatic nightmare, teaching me lessons not in the course syllabus.

I was employed full-time and convinced my employer to give me eight weeks' leave of absence. I flew to Thailand to study environmental ethics and social movements. What was I thinking? I was a 66-year-old baby-boomer about to study abroad with a group of 18 to 20-year-olds. Was I reliving my youth and ignoring the wrinkles on my face? I knew it could potentially be challenging to be socially accepted by individuals fifty years younger than me, but I had no idea how difficult it would be and how much pain it would cause.

About 15 young women from St. Louis journeyed to Thailand on the trip. Students from all over Asia were on campus: Bhutan, Nepal, Thailand, and more. Only the American girls and I took the field trip class that took us to Bangkok about two weeks after we had arrived. Those first two weeks were fine connecting with my classmates and learning the lay of the land. On the field trip however, we became stuck in a nightmare traffic jam on the way to our restaurant one evening. This was no ordinary traffic jam, but one where we would gain one car length every ten minutes. It became increasingly stressful in our van. The American girls in my van began talking and giggling about movie stars and celebrities. I tuned out, but after an hour or so, I became so bored I started to interject a conversation idea, asking the girls, "We have been learning about social entrepreneurship in our class, so what could we do back in Saint Louis with the concepts we have learned?" There was dead silence. I kept pressing it, and nobody responded. I should have shut up right then, but I continued, "What's the biggest problem in St. Louis we could affect?" Silence. I continued, "What if we had a cafe that could be run by white and Black women together, and it would be about social justice and bridging the divide?" Silence. Then, I made a colossal faux pas. I singled out the one African American student and asked her opinion. She responded, "I don't want to get involved in this conversation." After two miserable hours in that van, we finally arrived at the restaurant, and it began to dawn on me shortly afterward that I was being treated differently. Suddenly, I was a pariah. The next day, nobody talked to me- nobody. Somehow, I alienated the group. From that point forward, six more weeks to go, I was ostracized. I was persona non grata, and I didn't understand exactly what I said or did that offended them. I wasn't invited to any meals with them and rarely even received eye contact.

After a very traumatic first night when the realization hit me, I cried and cried and texted friends and supporters in the U.S., who gave me succor. I was ready to abort the trip then and there. On top of this, my daughter called from home to say our dog seemed to be sick, and I was so afraid we would lose our precious dog while I was stuck in Thailand, where I felt so alone.

But I bucked up and continued my studies in Thailand. I attended activities with expatriates who had retired in Thailand and people my age from the United States, Australia, Great Britain, and Canada. It was fun doing beach cleanups, hikes, and group dinners. However, that was only a couple of days out of the week. Most days, I would eat breakfast, lunch, and dinner all by myself.

I made a couple of friends on campus who were Asian students, so in a sense, my experience was more varied than the American "Mean Girls," as I came to call them. My experience was more diverse because I made the effort to meet expats and Asian students, yet I became incredibly homesick.

I was so delighted to get back on the plane to the United States and to recover from that trauma. My daughter, my friends, and my garden helped me to recover.

Then, a month later, I took my next class at the university on a September night. Twenty students and who should be in the class, but one of the "Mean Girls" from the Thailand trip. My heart sank.

The instructor started the class by discussing the distinction between 'calling people in' and 'calling people out.' When you 'call people out,' you tell them how wrong they are and criticize them. When you 'call people in,' you might explain why their words or communication style is problematic. Perhaps saying, "You know, the way you said that is problematic; I'd like to talk to you about that; I just challenge what you said, and here is why."

I thought 'calling people in" was a remarkable distinction and a great learning. After class, I emailed that one 'Mean Girl' student and asked her to meet me 15 minutes before the next class. I also asked her to 'call me in.' I wanted to learn what I did or said in Thailand that made me so outside the group. She agreed, and we met the following week before class. She was quite honest. I kept quiet and listened. She said that I was sometimes kind of demanding in class, saying, "Why aren't the Asian students speaking up instead of just all the American girls?" I talked a lot on the bus ride up there, and they found that annoying. Then, I was just a little too 'in your face' in how I communicated.

I could see how I was offending the young women. Her comments gave me time to reflect on how I was being and how my speaking was received by their listening. Her sharing with me helped me understand a little bit more, and I worked on my listening skills from that point on.

So, was I a victim of Mean Girls, or was I a loudmouth who voiced her opinions too aggressively? I think it is a bit of both. I do know that my study abroad in Thailand gave me a valuable education in humility and empathy. Although not in the course syllabus, some of the lasting lessons were totally unexpected.

Since my return, I have become more aware of how I interact with new groups of people, seeking to understand and be curious before voicing my opinions. I am cognizant of my proclivity to pontificate and catch myself if I start. I can 'call people in' in a caring way when what they say may be offensive.

In hindsight, my study abroad experience in Thailand was not merely an academic pursuit or adventure in a foreign country. Still, it provided an unexpected learning experience, my own journey of self-discovery.

Rebecca Now is an author, innovative historian, and performer with a passion for women's rights history.

She is the author of the award-winning book, "Borrowed Courage," which explores the journey of three 21st-century women, each of whom forged a bond and profound respect for a 19th-century women's rights pioneer. Rebecca developed a reenactment trio performing as Elizabeth Cady Stanton, Susan B. Anthony, and Sojourner Truth. Performers have been added, including Ida B. Wells and more.

The performances have evolved into a "talk show" format called "HERstory Comes to Life." Rebecca plays the host with a stage name of "Rebecca-Now-And-Then," where she introduces time-traveling guests from the past. She interviews them about their challenges and how they are stepping into their wisdom and power. Her non-profit, Voices of American HERstory, performs nationwide for community groups, national historical parks, schools, and more.

Rebecca loves her city of St. Louis, Missouri, and enjoys wellness, self-care, gardening, and cultural activities.

Please scan this QR code to connect with the author.

Gail Lee

Power, Purpose, and Resilience

Each time I faced a major adversity, I became stronger and even more resilient. I have thought back on many things, sometimes wishing they wouldn't have happened but knowing they have shaped my life and who I am. I appreciate those experiences because I like who I am. When deciding to write this, I thought I was an example of the power I have built through adversity. Telling my story can help other women navigate the obstacles through their families for generations.

In my early years, I had what most considered the typical family: Mom, Dad, siblings, and spending time with friends. I felt safe just exploring and learning. We had family vacations and trips, played in the neighborhood, went to church, visited family, and came home when the streetlights came on. This was the typical suburban upbringing. This provided good groundwork for my foundation.

When I started to have adversity, I could draw on that groundwork and support systems to overcome it. This background was where I drew my inner wisdom from and the direction on what to do next.

I grew up in my neighborhood going to the same school through 6th grade, and then my family moved to a new house, new school, and new friends.

Then, just before my 13th birthday, my mom died. It was very traumatic for me and my family. My mom had disappeared one evening and didn't return home. After she had been missing for a week, her body was found in the river. As a child, I was told she had been murdered. To say this caused a lot of trauma for myself, my siblings, and my dad is an understatement.

Many things have come up since then regarding what happened to my mom, but those are not so important for this to tell other than to say I have accepted that I will never know exactly what happened. Her death occurred, and it was hard. Through reflection, I am comfortable with not knowing and at peace with the unanswered questions. Suddenly as the oldest, I had to take on a lot of tasks for my younger brothers and help to make things in the house function. My dad had to be there for us, and I know this was so hard.

As an adult, I have experienced loss and grief and thought, how did my dad keep going, working, and supporting us as he did? There were plenty of criticisms of how my dad handled things, but being there for the front-row seat, he did a fantastic job. It wasn't perfect, but he was our constant example of determination and how to keep going.

I developed a solid framework of support from my church, family, and friends. I needed that during some of the chaos going on those first few years. My dad eventually got remarried to my "stepmom," whom I never really called that or thought of in that way. She was a solid presence in our lives for 50 years until she passed. She was truly my second mom. I feel blessed to have had both my mom's. I learned and was loved so much by both.

I graduated and was accepted to several colleges but took a different route that built resilience in my life. I joined the Army, and at the time, there weren't many women in the service. I entered Basic Combat Training

(BCT) 10 days after the Women's Army Corps (WAC) was disbanded and found myself in the first co-ed BCT unit at Ft. McClelland, the former home of the WAC headquarters. This was a huge cultural shift for the post, the drill sergeants, and all the participants involved. There were also many people of different cultures and races all thrown into this one living, working, traumatic experience. It helped inform me of white privilege and was the beginning of a journey for me of reconciliation and awareness of the struggles people experience. I was in the Army for eight years and worked as a behavioral science specialist, a counselor who helped other soldiers. Working in Social Work and counseling has been my goal since high school. I had turned down college acceptance due to family and financial concerns, but I still made my dream and goal happen in the Army. When I got out, I had my college degree and eight years of experience working in my career. I continued to work for the Department of the Army for 22 years and it shaped my work ethic.

During this period, I was married for 16 years and was in what I thought was a very solid marriage. We lived in various places across the country and the world. We worked and went to school together. I had finished a graduate degree and became a mom. Then, I went through a very difficult divorce, became a single parent, and had to choose to leave my government job.

Through a Base Realignment and Closure, I had to take severance or work at Ft. Leonard Wood, Missouri, which was 125 miles each way from my home. Driving daily was challenging if my daughter became sick at school and needed to come home. Picking her up put strains on the school and my job, having to leave abruptly and the long drive taking so much time to address the problem. It was a tough time because she had a previously undiagnosed eye disorder, suddenly causing daily issues in school. Due to some new custody laws in Missouri, I could not relocate her. I took these challenges head-on because I needed to do what was best for my daughter. I experienced a lot of challenges while bringing up my daughter. Being a single parent is just that, doing things alone.

After leaving the government and having reduced pay and benefits, I experienced an unexpected layoff, got a second master's degree to help with employment opportunities, and lost a fiancé. All these things can happen in life but handling them head-on and minimizing the effects on my daughter was always a priority.

These experiences were hard and challenging, but now I don't think of any of these things in life as horrible; they are obstacles, and I had to keep going. I learned to persevere. When I was having one of the lows in life, my second mom said something very comforting. She said my dad wasn't worried about me in these circumstances because he knew I would be okay and always come out on top. She said some things had happened to her in life, and as each one had happened, her resilience grew. She thought I had this determination and resilience, too, due to all the various circumstances in my life. Each of these challenges made me stronger.

From my adversity, I found myself wanting to help others. I wanted to be a social worker and did that in the military and afterward. I have continued to work in social services in various roles for my career. I have enjoyed this and have also been very involved in church, Lions Club, and other activities that help others. I wanted to help empower others to reach their potential without having as much adversity.

I also started a social service company a few years ago and have had people working for me to help others in our community.

I don't make a lot of money in this venture and don't personally get paid. Others have asked me on many occasions why you are doing this. Maybe you should just shut down. Is it worth the effort? I have trained and supported many people, and they have been supported financially along the way. It does feel good to help others. This allows me to continue looking forward and not dwell on adversity and those struggles.

Those challenges from growing up and throughout life have given me focus and determination to stay the course. I look at things optimistically and assume positive intent when reflecting on others' actions. I do not worry about things; I look forward to finding solutions to problems that come up. I look at what needs to be done and just work on it until it works, no matter what is thrown in the way.

Loss has been a theme in my life since my mother's death. It changed my "normal" childhood into one with challenges. There have been other losses and challenges in life, too. In addition to family and friends, my faith has always helped me navigate life's storms.

We were involved in church, and it was important to my parents. When she passed, the friends and church community surrounded me and helped me learn to get through things. The support provided stability and strength.

After my mom's death, faith continued to play such a big factor in my life. It was always there and helped me through life when I faced a storm or adversity. Through my faith in Christ, I have always known someone has been with me. Despite any type of loss, I am not alone. Knowing this has always given me the strength to pull from.

Faith has always been there and helped me through life when I faced a storm or adversity. Usually, with a storm, we face it with fear or faith. During life storms, we usually lose focus on Jesus' presence. There are many waves in life, and Jesus has always been there during those times. No matter what has happened, Jesus has been there, ultimately providing peace and bringing peace in life's storms and trials. I have always been able to find peace and tranquility in the presence of God, knowing the storm won't last and a beautiful sky will come if I hang in there.

Things are and have been in my power to resolve and get through any adversity, coming out stronger on the other end. I have consistently persevered, and life has shown me when I come through the other side and see that beautiful sky, I can continue toward my goals, those dreams, and aspirations. When I keep focus, I will persevere, enjoy my life, and feel peace.

Faith, family, friends, and community will always get me through. They are my strength and provide my focus, determination, and perseverance. They are my inner power.

Gail Lee is a noted expert on issues surrounding the care and treatment of the elderly and disabled. She has a Master's degree in Psychology and a Master's in Gerontology. She is a Missouri Licensed Clinical Social Worker (LCSW), a certified care manager (CCM), a certified employee assistance professional (CEAP), and an Illinois Licensed Clinical Professional Counselor (LCPC).

Currently, Gail serves as a Senior Advisor for Amen, Ganter, Capriano law firm in St. Louis, offering her expertise in asset protection planning and social service concerns of elderly clients. She is also the owner of A+ Aging Advantage, specializing in case management for elderly and disabled patients. Gail is the founder and President of Aging Advantage Inc., a non-profit organization dedicated to assisting Seniors in the community. She co-founded the nonprofit organization Elijah Moore Dreamer Fund, which has been providing scholarships to needy, disadvantaged students since 2009.

A proud U.S. Army Veteran, and dedicated mother and grandmother. Her role as a new grandmother has given her a fresh perspective on life and learning.

Please scan this QR code to connect with the author.

Karen Hoffman

My Power. My Wisdom.

Power. Definition: The capacity or ability to direct or influence the behavior of others or the course of events.

Wisdom. Definition: The body of knowledge and principles that develops within a specified society or period.

A recent discussion made me reflect on the words "power" and "wisdom" and what they mean to me. When I think of power or being powerful, I wonder: Where does power reside? Where does it come from? How do we develop power in ourselves?

For the first time, I had my own epiphany about power. Does power directly relate to our personal passion and our life purpose? Does uncovering our purpose and passion really help us discover our personal power, which, in turn, helps lead us to additional wisdom? I started by thinking about myself and my power. When did I begin to feel more powerful and become less fearful of speaking up? Did it have anything to do with uncovering my purpose and passions? I have felt more grounded since uncovering my purpose with our nonprofit, Gateway to Dreams, in 2014. Something internally shifted, and I felt different somehow.

Then I started thinking of my friends and associates… I thought of Rebecca Now, one of the organizers of this anthology. I've known Rebecca for many years and saw her evolve into someone who has become so "on purpose." When Rebecca mentioned her interest in taking on the persona/reenactor role of Elizabeth Cady Stanton, a woman I had never heard of, Rebecca became more excited and alive. Rebecca really wanted others to learn and see the significant role Elizabeth played in our history. While many of us know about Susan B. Anthony and her significance for women's rights, Elizabeth and Susan were an inseparable force. It was fascinating to watch Rebecca own her personal power by becoming a historical reenactor of Elizabeth Cady Stanton. Rebecca had her period costume created, set a date for her first speech, invited people, and hosted her first event portraying Elizabeth Cady Stanton. She took action, and as her power emerged, her wisdom grew, and she researched all she could about Elizabeth. Rebecca has become a historian of sorts with her own reenactment team. Power and wisdom go hand in hand.

Another woman who has become more powerful and gained much wisdom is a dear friend, Rosemary Britts. We met during a workshop I was hosting, and Rosemary shared a goal to start an association to help families. She displayed little confidence in herself as she created a goal to research and possibly start a nonprofit. The nonprofit would be focused on sickle cell disease, educating those with sickle cell and their families. Her daughter, Ronica, or as she was affectionately known, "Ro," was born with sickle cell, and Rosemary was determined to learn everything she could about the disease for her daughter and other families. One of her first stops was to discuss her idea of an association for sickle cell at the hospital where her daughter was being treated. The hospital had been waiting for her to commit to helping them, and they were ready to support her with money and resources. Rosemary took this on, and I watched her power grow, fueled by her purpose and passion. Power also, to me, looks like confidence. Her power and confidence increased. The wisdom, knowledge about sickle cell disease, starting a nonprofit, and applying for grants all contributed to making her a wiser woman. Power and wisdom go hand in hand.

Another person I watched gain personal power was Dr. Marty K. Casey. When I first met Marty, I was enthralled by her on-stage persona— so authentic and relatable. Marty is an actor and singer who created the word "actorvist" to describe her life as both an actor and an activist. That day, I joined the speakers, including Marty, for a private lunch. I then initiated a conversation to learn more about the people in the room and what we might do to support them and their work. When we got to Dr. Marty, she revealed more of who she was. Being in St. Louis, where most of us lived, Marty talked about the rioting after Michael Brown was shot. Marty had her revelation that rioting would not be the answer to racial issues. Marty then reflected on her OWN life. She looked at how she rose above poverty and chaos, using her voice and music. Despite being expelled and suspended from multiple schools, Marty had a gift for singing, which was recognized by her music teacher from Webster Groves High School. This teacher saw Marty's anger and rebellion and advised her to change her negative attitude and use her voice. Marty took this advice to heart, and during the rioting, she recognized that maybe, just maybe, she could help kids like her channel their passions into the arts, primarily singing, to keep them off the streets. As we ate lunch, Marty shared the places where her kids went to sing and act as part of her Show Me Arts Academy. Marty started realizing the effects of generational trauma and violence in our city were tied together. Marty started working with teens AND adults to help them UnGun emotionally. While Marty was already a powerful woman as her work continued, her power and wisdom combined to help her help people in St. Louis and globally. Dr. Marty K. Casey used her power and wisdom, much like Dr. Martin Luther King, to spread love and healing. Marty reminds me of a female Dr. Martin Luther King. Her power. Her wisdom.

My power. My wisdom. I want to share how I gained additional wisdom and created a more powerful way of being. When I started Gateway to Dreams, I invited entrepreneurial friends to help me brainstorm what our nonprofit could become. I now call this group our "Launch Ambassadors." We met weekly from July until we hosted our first fundraiser in October. We started just wanting to help people with their dreams and goals. We hosted a monthly Dream Fest with coaches and guests. We brainstormed for each person in attendance. We also had a monthly speaker, usually a nonprofit, who would share their story and what they needed. As we expanded into a larger space, we added additional programs. As we grew, there were many ups and downs, and I learned to trust that we would make the right decision and that things would always work out.

I recently learned a lesson about inclusivity that has impacted me on several levels. Have you ever considered the issues surrounding inclusivity? Have you ever considered what you could do to impact inclusivity? I had not. Part of my personality loves connecting with people. I always reach out to as many members of our nonprofit and guests as possible before our monthly member meetings to invite them and remind them about an upcoming meeting. I reach out via email, text, or Facebook Messenger. Looking back over the last 10 years, I learned to differentiate between "accidental inclusion" and "intentional inclusion."

Initially, I invited all my friends, and because the majority of attendees were white, I would invite anyone I thought of. Then, I became deliberate about inviting as many of my friends of color to our nonprofit events as possible and recognizing them as potential speakers—purposeful and deliberate inclusion. Now, our community is more diverse, which I love.

Now, I always work to be inclusive on purpose. Using my personal power to connect in a deliberate way also means using my wisdom.

Personal things I have learned about power and wisdom:

1. Our personal powers are tied to our purpose and passions.

2. Wisdom comes from learning new things and being open. I believe wisdom is to be shared.

3. My experience is that power and wisdom are not static traits but dynamic qualities that evolve through purposeful action, purpose, passion, and a commitment to learning.

I hope my reflections can serve as a guide in seeking to understand and develop your personal power and wisdom.

Karen Hoffman is a visionary entrepreneur and the driving force behind Gateway to Dreams, a non-profit organization based in St. Louis, Missouri.

With a passion for empowering individuals to reach their full potential, Karen founded Gateway to Dreams to provide resources, education, and support to help people achieve their personal and professional dreams.

As a seasoned business leader, Karen brings a wealth of expertise in entrepreneurship, coaching, and community development to her role as the executive director of Gateway to Dreams. Under her guidance, the organization has become a beacon of hope and inspiration for many in the St. Louis area.

Karen's dedication to making a positive impact on the community is evident in Gateway to Dreams' innovative programs and initiatives, which continue to uplift and transform lives.

Please scan this QR code to connect with the author.

Linda Robinson

My Authentic Self: No More Mask

I thought I was a Superwoman. No one or nothing could break me. Then I had a mental meltdown. Why am I talking about this topic? I know for sure other women, especially Black (Biracial) women, have felt or experienced the same things I have, and your outcome depends on who you pull your strength from.

During the last five years of working in the corporate world, I experienced micromanagement, gaslighting, a toxic environment, and unprofessionalism from upper management to the team members. Sometimes, I did not know if I was in a professional or high school environment. I always had to prove myself and have it all together. As a Black woman with white management, I had to work harder to get my point across and show management I knew what I was talking about regarding updating procedures, working with other departments, and our day-to-day work.

My attitude and behavior about going to work was so negative, and I despised going to the office. I would pray before leaving home, sit in my car, and listen to gospel music to give me the power and right mind frame to deal with the people. The entire team was not toxic, but the ones who were…OMG is all I can say. Even though I would pray daily, my attitude and negativity blocked my blessing from moving forward. God knew He had to change me within before I could receive my true blessing from Him.

One day, I could not take it anymore. I called Human Resources and filed a complaint against my management and a few team members. The HR representative mentioned that I should take a "stress leave" leave to take time and relax. I was like no way!! Not me. I got this. I cannot have time off from work because I am stressed. I might take time off here and there, but not a leave of absence from work. She said that with my years of service, I could take off several weeks with pay and keep my benefits. I brushed it off and never thought about it again.

Months later, it was time for my annual physical. The nurse took my blood pressure and said it was higher than usual. She said I would need to retake it just to sit and relax. My doctor came in, and she retook my blood pressure, which was still higher than usual. She asked, "Are you okay? What is going on in your life?"

I broke down and cried like I did when I lost my mom. I cried so hard that I could not even talk to my doctor. I told the doctor my job was stressing me out, and I could not work there anymore. I did not know what to do. I had been looking for a new job, and nothing was happening.

My doctor put me on leave from work and told me to call my manager to let her know. She promised to sign and send the necessary forms to my employer ASAP. She also recommended I see a therapist. "What? I do not need to see a therapist. I got this," I thought.

Wow, I still could not believe I had taken a leave of absence from work due to stress. Let me tell you why I was that person. I grew up with a Korean mom who always told us we are strong, do not show anyone we are weak, and we have tiger blood. That meant I was strong and could conquer anyone or anything. All my life, I had to be strong and smile. My mom taught me to depend on God. "Plus, I got this," is what I was still telling myself.

I did reach out to the therapist my doctor recommended. I had so many doubts about seeing a therapist because of stress. I met with one after I lost my mom, but not for stress!! The therapist helped me to know that I did not have to walk around like I was Superwoman or have it all together. I realized it was okay NOT to be OK. My mental health was just as important as my physical health. When the therapist prescribed medication to help with anxiety, I was conflicted. At first, I thought, "I am not taking this little white pill; I've got God." Then I would counter that with, "Come on, Linda, take the pill. It is okay to take the pill and see a therapist. You are not alone. Here you go again, trying to manage things on your own."

Prayer and therapy helped me when I lost my mom in 2003 and when I needed a leave of absence in 2018. I could not have foreseen how much I would rely on both again in 2019.

On October 24, 2019, my brother Mark came to tell us he loved and hugged us. It was the last time I would see him or hear his voice. I knew something was wrong, but I was too focused on meetings for work and ignored the feeling. That afternoon, I received a phone call and learned Mark had not come to work. After my meeting, I checked on him and found him unresponsive and cold. My brother had taken his life. I felt so much guilt and blamed myself.

I had felt pain before, but this pain was unbearable and broke me into pieces, and I had to lean and trust God wholeheartedly to get me through.

I wished I had taken the time to speak with him because something was wrong that morning. When he was hospitalized and connected to every machine to keep him alive, I prayed and asked God to give him rest and let our family be okay. Death is always hard on a family, but death by suicide is a pain I cannot explain. I pray no one must experience losing someone they love this way.

I prayed and attended GriefShare, a grief support group, to help me deal with the loss and pain. This was indeed a step to my healing and understanding of grief and how to cope with it. I also found a therapist who specialized in grief to help me as I was learning to live without Mark and move forward.

Therapy helped me realize that being happy is being our true, authentic selves, flaws and all. It is okay to take off the mask and let everyone see us shine.

I discovered the effects of praying and meditating on God's words. I studied the Bible to encourage, strengthen, and guide me. I exercised at the gym and walked outside. That is when I discovered nature and how therapeutic it can be. I learned that self-care is essential, and I started journaling.

As I started building my relationship with God, I sought Him for guidance. I talked to Him about my life and where and what to do next. That is when God started helping me understand vibes and energy from others. I learned to trust my intuition and know that if it does not feel right, it is not.

Overcoming these challenges helped me understand who I am, whose I am, my self-worth, and my power, and that my self-esteem and confidence are unstoppable. My voice matters regardless of how anyone takes it or how they feel afterward. I realize the power of saying "NO" and not feeling bad about it. I schedule my self-care, and it feels so good. I have been rejuvenated and revived, and I am living the life that God has for me and not what others want me to be. I am not weak, but I am not a Superwoman.

I encourage you to take care of yourself. Own who you are and be happy. Be you and be true to yourself. Love who you are and embrace yourself 100%. Always let God lead you. If you need professional help, seek it. Go to the therapist, take the pill, find a mentor, and keep your circle tight with loving, caring, and God-fearing individuals. Smile and tell yourself that "God has got me." I no longer say, "I got this," because God showed me who truly has me and who I can call on 24/7. I am awake, and it feels so good. I love and cherish Linda Robinson wholeheartedly. She is so amazing!

Being strong, never saying "no," and giving myself to everyone else but to myself was not good for me or my self-care. You cannot pour from an empty cup!

During the pandemic, we had to wear masks to protect ourselves. I continue to wear a mask physically, but my mask is off mentally, and I am showing you my true, authentic self. What you see is what you get. I am no longer making sure everyone and everything is okay. I am not doing it if it does not align with me mentally, emotionally, or spiritually. If it is out of my hands, it is out of my control. I rely on God's timing. He is in control, and his plan is better than mine. God got me!!

Linda Robinson is Advisor-Area Director at ALSAC St. Jude, the fundraising and awareness organization for St. Jude Children's Research Hospital.

Her educational background includes a Bachelor of Science in Communication specializing in Public Relations from Lindenwood University and two master's degrees, one in Human Resource Development and Nonprofit Management from Webster University.

A passionate champion for mental health, mental illness, and suicide prevention, Linda serves as a family support group facilitator for the National Association of Mental Illness–STL and advocates for the American Foundation for Suicide Prevention.

Her extensive community and civil commitments include the Hatz 4 Hearts Foundation, Maplewood-Richmond Heights School District Board of Education, Webster University's African American Alumni Chapter, and the Alumni Association. Linda serves on the St. Louis County Human Relations Commission, Maplewood Civil Service Commission, Board of Adjustment, and Housing Boards of Appeal.

A dedicated mother and grandmother, Linda is also a member of Friendly Temple Church.

Please scan this QR code to connect with the author.

Phyllis A. Williams

A Soldier's Story

My journey toward service and leadership started before I became a strong woman with lots of wisdom. It may have started before I was old enough to realize it.

I grew up in a family of 10 siblings: six girls and four boys. From oldest to youngest were Dorothy, Jimmie, Pete, me, Emma, Rosie, Earskia, Jeffrey, Marilyn, and Darline. Emma, Jeffrey, and Marilyn are deceased. We were loving and kind and helped each other when needed.

My parents moved us from Mobile, Alabama, to St. Louis, Missouri, in 1965. Jeff and Vannie Cook were very loving and devoted parents. They were always there for all of us. Their unconditional love taught us that we could be whatever we wanted. Dad was a mechanic, and Mom was a homemaker. They taught us that getting an education was very important. Our dad was always on time for work. This is how life was modeled for me before I ever knew anything about what it took to be successful.

We only had one bathroom, so at 5 a.m. every morning, my dad would be up and getting ready for work. I would sit on the steps to be the first in after he came out. When I got fully dressed and went downstairs, my mother had breakfast ready, and my dad would have already eaten and was headed out the door. This was an amazing example of how my mother and father worked together as a loving husband and wife and as great parents. This was my foundation and integral to becoming the person I wanted to be.

I was 12 when Dad bought me a typewriter and asked me to write a letter. I learned all the keys so I could type faster. Whenever he asked me to type a letter, I could finish it without error and return to playing.

After graduating from Sumner High School, I attended Harris Stowe Teacher College. My dad helped me financially for one semester. After that, I did not know what I was going to do. I heard the military motto, "Be all you can be, join the Army," which stuck in my mind and guided me to join the Army.

Although I was only four feet eleven inches, many professions wanted a bigger and stronger person. I did not let my height hold me back, and I joined the Army Reserve in 1979 and went on active duty in 1982. I had many challenges throughout my career but never let my size get in the way. I could do as many pushups and run as fast as the guys in my platoon.

My strength, tenacity, and resilience earned me several awards, including the Legion of Merit, Southwest Asia Pacific Award, Kuwait Liberation Medal, Joint Meritorious Award, Meritorious Service Medal with four oak leaf clusters, Global War on Terrorism Award, and the National Defense Service Medal.

Challenges.

In basic training, during our weapon training, I scored expert on my M16. The training was intense, but I never gave up, which impressed my first sergeant. I could also type more than one hundred words per minute. He wanted the letters to be fast and without errors. I could and did accomplish that task. He reminded me of my dad.

I always set realistic goals for myself. I grew in wisdom and faith as I met each objective and believed in my abilities.

My command sergeant major always sought someone to take charge or lead the physical training and other important duties. I never backed down from a challenge. I ran our physical training for many years. Soldiers had to stay physically fit and in shape. We tested at least twice a year.

I focused on my growth and wisdom and never worried about measuring up to anyone else's standard. I knew my strengths and abilities, and that's how I continued to get promoted and earn the respect of my peers and the command.

My biggest supporters all my career were my late husband, Sergeant Major Robert S. Williams, and my son Ronnie. Ronnie is a military brat who never complained when I had to leave him with other family members as a child. He was in high school when I was deployed to Saudi Arabia.

Quotes by President John F. Kennedy and Gen. Colin Powell affirmed my commitment and service to our country. "Ask not what your country can do for you. Ask what you can do for your country" is still an often-cited quote by our 35th president.

Gen. Colin Powell was the first Reserve Officer Training Corps (ROTC) graduate at an early age. He played a central role in preparation for the Persian Gulf War. During Operation Desert Storm, my unit, the 416th Engineer Command, was deployed and operated under Gen. Powell's leadership from 1990 to '91. His quote, "All work is honorable. Always do your best because someone is watching," resonated with me throughout my career.

The military taught me to be honest and strong and never give up. I was highly respected in the Army because of my dedication to the mission and wisdom. During Desert Shield/Desert Storm, I mentored and guided my young soldiers. We performed our jobs and missions on the highest level.

Throughout my military journey, I have met some fantastic and professional men and women. They could have chosen many careers but decided to serve their country. My drill sergeant was a powerful and dedicated female soldier. I highly respected her leadership and dedication. This also helped me build bridges and opportunities for myself. With every promotion in the Army, my wisdom and knowledge expanded. The Army constantly sent me to classes to ensure I had the tools to be a great leader. I took a nuclear biological chemical course. This class was demanding, but I was highly prepared when deployed to Saudi Arabia. The course taught me to share my knowledge, experience, and field training. During Desert Storm, I taught classes on how to wear Mission-Origin Protective Posture (MOPP) suits. It prepared me to lead and guide my soldiers. Because of our headquarters operations, we were in an area of contamination or imminent threat. We had to wear our MOPP suits constantly.

I was an equal opportunity advisor for the United States Army. I made sure that the workforce maintained hiring and employment practices untainted by bias based on race, gender identity, age, and national origin.

After 28 years in the Army, I decided to retire. I taught Junior Reserve Officer Training Corps (JROTC) at the Ferguson–Florissant School District when I retired. I was excited to teach during my first week of school because this was new. I taught students from ninth through twelfth grade. My job was to help develop cadets to perform as highly as possible and become good citizens. I worked harder than ever to help mold these cadets into our future leaders. I was given the position of Senior Advisor. I also had a first sergeant to work as my advisor. He was stern, and I was delighted to work with him.

The cornerstone of JROTC was our leadership training and development. It helped teenagers gain character abilities, leadership, and life skills to apply in their education, career, and life. The JROTC class was very demanding, but many cadets liked it. When they stayed long enough, they could appreciate what it offered. The core elements of JROTC are citizenship, leadership, character, and community service. Also, it instills in them self-esteem, teamwork, and self-discipline. Many of my cadets have gotten outstanding jobs, and some have gone into the military.

I am currently a substitute teacher in the Fort Zumwalt School District. This is also a new chapter in my life, and it is very challenging because I'm still working with students and molding them.

Once again, the same motto guides me: "Be all you can be." I have been retired for 17 years. The Soldier's Creed, which I lived by for 28 years, still provides me with a framework as I move toward my life's new chapters and opportunities.

The Army Creed:

1. I am an American soldier.

2. I am a warrior and a member of a team.

3. I serve the people of the United States and live the military values.

4. I always place the mission first.

5. I will never accept defeat.

6. I would never quit.

7. I will never leave a fallen comrade.

8. I am disciplined physically and mentally tough.

9. Trained and proficient in my warrior tasks and drills.

10. Always maintain my arms, my equipment, and myself.

11. I am an expert, and I am a professional.

12. I stand ready to deploy, engage, and destroy the enemies of the United States of America in close combat.

13. I'm a guardian of freedom and the American way of life.

14. I am an American soldier.

Phyllis A. Williams is a retired Master Sergeant (MSG) in the United States Army with 28 years or service. She is also a retired (JROTC) Junior Reserve Officer Corp Teacher, from the Ferguson Florissant School District of Eight years of dedicated service. Phyllis has one devoted son Ronald Harris. She was married to the late Sergeant Major Robert S Williams (RIP). They have 4 grandkids and 11 great grands.

Phyllis holds a Master's degree in Human Resource Management. (Magna cum laude) and a Bachelor of Arts degree in Sociology. Her military career has moved her to many states and out of the country. She was stationed in Seoul Korea and Baumholder Germany. She was deployed during Desert Shield Desert Storm 1990-91, with the 416th. Engineer Command. Phyllis abilities makes her a force ready to impact the world. Her mission in life is to influence and unlock her strength and Creativity. Through her dedication to her soldiers and students, she has mentored them with unwavering dedication and perseverance.

Please scan this QR code to connect with the author.

Kathleen Martin and Tia Adkins

Something in Common

Kathleen:

Michael Brown had been tragically killed on the street in Ferguson, and the whole St. Louis area was on edge. As a white lady, I was struck by how little I was aware of how my Black sisters and brothers were impacted by racial prejudice in their everyday lives.

A group of eleven women, six white and five Black, met in the conference room at my church. The white women knew each other from a Bible Study group; each Black woman knew only one of the white women. We agreed that we wanted to do something to bridge the racial divide, but we had no specific plan. When I awoke at night, God was clear about what he wanted. He wanted us to be in a relationship with one another, building on our common relationship with Him. This was not to be a "one-and-done event," but meeting together regularly to develop our relationships.

As I looked in the mirror the next morning, what I saw may have looked like me, but it sure didn't feel like what I was experiencing. In my mind's eye, I saw two figures hovering over my shoulders, with a devil on one side and an angel on the other. As I stared at my reflection, I asked myself, "What are you thinking? You can't possibly pull this off during the holiday season." Thanksgiving was coming up next week, and Christmas was just four short weeks after. The response came from a different voice. "You're right, Kathleen, you can't. I can! So, move your feet."

The prayer we pray in church asking forgiveness for the "things done and things left undone" resonated in that moment.

Our first event in mid-December was attended by a racially mixed group of 28 women. It included a dinner, a faith-based speaker, a break-out discussion, and singing. The model of coming together bi-monthly with a different program and meeting in different parts of the metropolitan area continued after that. One of the hallmarks of these workshops was the opportunity to discuss topics on which we had different experiences based on our race.

We started with the slogan "Made in God's Image" and soon branded ourselves Sisters CARE (Christians Advocating Racial Equality). We grew to have over 300 women on our distribution list.

Tia:

It has been said that Sunday at 10:00 a.m. is the most segregated hour of the week. I remember the first time I met Kathleen Martin. I was invited to participate in a Sisters CARE workshop. Kathleen and other Christian women founded it after the death of Michael Brown in 2014. The idea was that these women who had their Christian faith in common would work with other women of different races who were also Christians to get together to do something to try to restore the peace in the city. We wanted to make sure that St. Louis could be viewed as something other than a killing field of death and destruction and a city with the highest crime rate in the country.

So, what did these women think that they could do? I believe we thought that by banding together in faith and a common Christian expe-rience, we could get to know one another and do something to change the perception of the city. I believe we thought we would be picketing, marching, and doing something to express our unity and how love and faith in God can solve any problems that humans have with one another. We thought that we would be an action group. Although we didn't know each other, with a common cause, we could unite and make a difference. I think some women started with great enthusiasm, but they didn't understand what would happen.

I listened to these loving, faithful, and earnest women trying to acquaint themselves with their sisters in Christ. They wanted to understand and get to know each other better as Christians who worshiped in different styles and parts of the city. They exhibited discipline and quiet energy of developing relationships. Personally, I experienced their encouragement when they attended my comedy contests and their love and support after a serious accident.

We cannot legislate our way out of 400 years of trial and tribulation. What must happen is that we have to get to know and trust one another.

Kathleen:

As Tia began to attend Sisters CARE workshops, it was clear that she was ready to jump in with both feet. Soon, she suggested she would enjoy meeting with the other ladies in a setting with no agenda, just time to get to know each other better. Some of the other ladies also expressed a desire for a less structured time together. We started meeting monthly on Saturday mornings for coffee, and Tia suggested we call these "Chick Chats." As you can imagine, the Chick Chats quickly became popular. Often, events in the media became the topic of conversation. This presented the opportunity for us to share and appreciate different perspectives.

One evening, we sat at a discussion table during a Sisters CARE workshop after watching the movie, "Hidden Figures," as a group. One of the protocols at a Sisters CARE workshop was that each discussion group must be racially mixed. If you are unfamiliar with "Hidden Figures," it is an inspiring movie based on the true story of three African-American women working for NASA. They served as the brains behind one of the greatest operations in history: the launch of astronaut John Glenn into orbit. It illustrates the determination and perseverance needed to overcome racist and misogynistic attitudes.

The topic at that point centered around the fact that Al Harrison had not eliminated the segregated bathrooms in real life as the Kevin Costner character portrayed in the movie.

"Well, I can tell you this: she must have had a white advocate," a regular participant said about the Katherine Goble Johnson character in "Hidden Figures," played by Taraji P. Henson. She is a Black aeronautical engineer working for an aerospace company like Ms. Johnson. Her point was there was poetic license taken in the movie, but it dramatically showed that advocacy was in play.

Tia:

After all these years of participating in Sister CARE, I have become friends with some of the women with whom I don't share much background except humanity and Christianity. The most revolutionary thing you can do is get to know someone else's point of view. Searching for the commonality in humans is a good thing to do. Building relationships with your fellow human beings is a good thing to do. It is through building these relationships that we become advocates for one another, not just marching but knowing one another.

Kathleen:

It was October 2017, and I was participating in a mixed-race group discussing touchy topics. The person responsible for the topic that week talked about the travesty of celebrating Columbus Day. We also watched an episode of the TV series "Blackish," in which the characters re-enacted their idea of what it was like for a black family in Texas in 1865 to learn they were no longer enslaved. The idea arose that we should have a June-teenth celebration.

I worked feverishly with a team organizing the celebration, arranging catering, the location, entertainment, speakers, news media, etc. The idea was that the Black presenters and entertainers would be the face of the event. This is the reverse of slavery, where the slaves did all the work, and the credit went to the white owners. (Can anyone really own another person?)

I had to reflect on my past behavior, instances where I may have been an advocate, and times when I wasn't. There was the time when I agreed to rescue a project that was bleeding money daily. I was able to bring on a Black co-worker who aspired to be a project manager and have her manage the project once I mentored her and brought the project back on track. Fortunately, the company we worked for was interested in promoting qualified minorities, so the sell was easy. After managing that project, she had a very successful career as a project management professional.

In another situation, I hired a young man from a southern city who didn't have the experience to be a consultant, but he did have experience in a hard-to-find subject area. He had been a college football player and was working at the university from which he graduated. Other people who had worked with him said he showed great promise. When I hired him, I ensured he had all the training and support he needed in the business operations. On his first assignment, he was mentored by a seasoned consultant with expertise in that subject area. Five years later, after I left the consulting company, I received a LinkedIn message from him telling me he would never forget me and the opportunity I had given him.

I could stop there and pat myself on the back. Unfortunately, there was another situation where I could have been more supportive of my Black teammate. He was a young father of two boys and the only non-white on the team. His job function on the team was more technical than the other team members. There were challenges with the quality of his work, and when we had to make a staff cut, he was the one who was easiest to let go. As I reflect on the situation, I realize that I could have done more to offer him assistance to improve his performance. I'm sure he was hesitant to admit the need for help. He didn't socialize much with the rest of the team; he probably had enough of being around white people all day at work. This is a case of my sin of omission.

One thing I learned is that white persons cannot call themselves allies for persons of color. That distinction can only be bestowed by a person of color.

Tia:

After all this time of knowing Kathleen, there is nothing that someone outside of our relationship can tell me about her. Because we are in relationship, I trust her. We've broken bread together, gone to activities together, and are friends.

I think it is important to remember that we are all one and that we are children of God. Spiritually, none of us are any different. Under the skin that we are in, we are all the same. There are systems in place that are interested in keeping us in conflict with one another. People are suspicious of that which they do not know.

When I went to college for the first time, I met white people who had never met Black people. I grew up in integrated spaces, and there was no time when I wasn't aware and in a relationship with white people. So, the idea that there were people who had never seen Black people in person was shocking to me. I suppose that college was the first time I realized there was a responsibility not to be stereotypical. It wasn't so much that I felt I held the responsibility for the entire race on my back, but maybe I felt that I did. Some things happened that truly angered me, but when

I realized that they were done out of ignorance and not malice, I made it my business to temper my responses. When white people would rub my skin or touch my hair without asking permission, part of me wanted to smack their hands away. I knew an adverse response from the only Black person they had ever encountered would give them a reason to think that all Black people were rude, easily angered, and violent. Knowledge is power, and what I knew was that all white people were not like the igno-ramuses who were touching me without permission.

Joint perspective:

It is worth the investment of doing the work to dissolve the prejudices we all carry. While this situation originated with Black and White prejudices, it applies to all races and backgrounds.

Kathleen Martin lives with her husband in suburban St. Louis, where she likes to hang out with her family and grandchildren. After retiring from a career as a project manager in the technology industry, she organizes Sisters CARE events and volunteers at church and with the Service Corps of Retired Executives (SCORE). She is the author of the children's book Abe's Bear Adventure, available on Amazon. She enjoys hiking and skiing in Montana.

Tia Adkins lives in a suburb of St. Louis and serves as a minister and preacher at the Center for Divine Love. She retired after a successful career as a Guest Services Manager at the Missouri Botanical Garden and Director of Guest Services at the Missouri History Museum. As a member of Toastmasters, her comedy performances received a number of awards. She portrays Sojourner Truth in the film *"Bringing HERstory to Life: Chats with 19th and 20th-Century Women."*

Oh, how good and pleasant it is when brethren live together in unity.
Psalm 133: 1

Please scan this QR code to connect with Kathleen Martin.

Elaine Curry

Breaking Barriers: A Woman's Journey in Corporate America

"It's a Man's World" is a song by James Brown and Betty Jean Newsome. Brown recorded it on February 16, 1966, in a New York City studio and released it as a single later that year.

Brown's words accurately represented the corporate climate when I started my career in the 1970s. It was a man's world, and though it would take years, those words would eventually prove antiquated!

I was born in the borough of Manhattan in Harlem Hospital, New York, New York. September 16, 1953. This is where my story begins.

I was oblivious to the obstacles that were awaiting me in life. As an African American (then we were called Negro), segregation was the way of life. In my early years, I didn't understand all the rights that I was denied due to the color of my skin. I would only understand much later in life. However, that was not the only obstacle I would face. I was a woman. It took a long time to learn that some doors would not be opened as it was a man's world!

In 1973, I embarked on my professional journey when I joined Merrill Lynch in Tacoma, Washington. Securing this position felt like a dream come true, as I was chosen to work as a bookkeeper in the back-office operations. My responsibilities included matching billing transactions to stock exchange activities. My department supervisor, with 13 years of experience, quickly recognized my aptitude and trusted me to take charge in her absence.

One day, the operations manager called me into his office to commend my performance. What he revealed next was both shocking and enlightening. He said, "When I requested a reference from your supervisor at the U.S. Post Office, I tossed it out because I saw that he was Mexican, and I don't trust them. I see I was right." His words were a harsh reminder of the prejudice I had faced earlier in my career.

At the post office, my supervisor unjustly terminated me after he approved my leave over Thanksgiving weekend. A pink notice awaited me upon my return, and when I sought clarification, he explained that new employees were not entitled to Thanksgiving leave. Despite acknowledging his mistake, he insisted the termination couldn't be reversed. My appeal to Human Resources yielded the same outcome: my file was closed.

As I left the HR area, I noticed the Office of the Postmaster General. Desperate for justice, I requested a meeting. The secretary arranged an appointment, and I was granted a meeting one week later. When I entered the room, I found myself facing four white men sitting at a table who were greeting me with an intimidating stare. I can assure you that I probably was paled by the setting and looked like the fifth white person in the room. They gestured for me to take a seat opposite them. They asked me to explain why I had requested the meeting. I gathered my courage and explained my situation. After hearing my story, I noticed them reviewing a folder that apparently was the story given to them by the supervisor who had requested my termination. They said that the report from my supervisor indicated that I had poor performance and was an excessive talker. I knew these claims were completely unfounded. I requested that he be brought into the meeting so that I could confront these allegations face-to-face.

The panel took a moment to confer with each other and returned to the table, stating that they had decided to dismiss his complaints and reinstate me on a six-week probationary period.

I was placed back under the same supervisor and worked diligently as I had before the incident. He frequently would stop at my workstation and praise my performance. I remained at the Post Office for another 18 months until I resigned. I left California for Tacoma, Washington, a year and a half later. However, little did I know that my supervisor continued to provide negative references about me when requested by future potential employers. Had the operations manager at Merrill Lynch not mentioned this, I might have continued struggling to find employment, confused by repeated rejections despite positive interviews.

This experience taught me a crucial lesson in self-confidence, the importance of standing up for myself, and the importance of not being weakened because I was a woman. It was the first of many obstacles I overcame on my climb to power as a woman in a male-dominated industry.

Fast-forward to 1994. Merrill Lynch Banque Suisse in Geneva, Switzerland, was embarking on restructuring the bank's operations and technology. They recruited various branch operations leaders from their international branches in Europe to participate in the team, selecting those with a customer base of Swiss bank accounts under the supervision of different international branches. I was chosen to be on this team. I commuted for a year between Frankfurt, Germany, and Geneva, Switzerland.

Upon completion of the restructuring, there was a need to hire someone to lead Merrill Lynch Banque Suisse's newly created operations and technology structure. To my amazement, I was one of the candidates. The chairman of the bank contacted me for an interview. I agonized over whether I was up for the challenge. My initial response was to reject the offer because I had finally settled comfortably in Germany and didn't feel ready to move to a new country and face adjustments similar to those I experienced when I first moved to Germany.

A few weeks later, the chairman called again to discuss the offer further. I will never forget the wonderful meal and first-class treatment at the country club. He explained that I was highly recommended for the position. I could hardly believe it, considering I knew two highly qualified Swiss banking operations individuals were also candidates. Now, I faced the dilemma of what would happen if I turned it down again.

Two things happened that influenced my decision. First, the branch manager's secretary in Frankfurt recounted how she turned down an opportunity for a career move that she later regretted. She urged me to seriously consider this chance for my career. Second, this role would elevate me and help me penetrate the glass ceiling that existed for women to get into the directorship at a Swiss bank. After much prayer, I accepted the job. In 1994, I was appointed a director of Merrill Lynch Banque Suisse, and my role was second only to the bank chairman.

This move had a profound impact, empowering me and opening doors. It positioned me in a role that demanded respect everywhere I represented the bank. I remained in that role for seven years before retiring from Merrill Lynch in 2001. However, I stayed in Switzerland and was soon contacted by an attorney, a former employee who had moved to another Swiss bank. His bank was searching for someone to head their operations, and he thought of me. I came out of retirement and worked another six years in Switzerland before deciding to return to the United States in 2007.

Upon my return to the U.S., I began working with Wachovia Securities in Richmond, VA., which had recently purchased a brokerage institution in St. Louis, MO. I was invited to move to St. Louis, joined what is now Wells Fargo Advisors, and retired again in 2017.

I attribute my success as a woman in power to being confident in who I am and my capabilities. Don't get discouraged; continue to jump the hurdles. Being a woman did not diminish me. Be empowered! Your intelligence does not have a gender, nor does your success. It is personal to you, the human being. Walk in the empowerment of gifts and talents.

Elaine Curry, a renowned speaker who motivates and inspires, is a member of Toastmasters International and belongs to their club, St. Clair Toastmasters, based in Belleville, IL.

She has held prestigious positions in Toastmasters, such as a Region Advisor (2021-2022) and a District Director (2019-2020) at Toastmasters International.

After dedicating 43 years to the Financial Services industry, she retired in January 2017 from her then-employer, Wells Fargo Advisors, in St. Louis, MO. Elaine notably spent 13 years as a Swiss bank director in Geneva, Switzerland, showcasing her expertise in international finance. Fluent in German and French, Elaine has worked extensively in Germany and Switzerland for 28 years, contributing significantly to her global perspective.

Aside from her professional achievements, Elaine is actively involved in the community. Since 2007, she has been a member of the Board of Directors for ASK-All Special Kids, a Swiss non-profit organization in Geneva.

Additionally, Elaine brings a spiritual dimension to her work as an ordained Minister and former Senior Pastor of Outreach Deliverance Center Church in Geneva, Switzerland, for twelve years.

Family-oriented, Elaine shares her life with her husband Lemont, two children, and five grandchildren. Together, they enjoy traveling, connecting with new people, and pursuing personal development goals in retirement.

Please scan this QR code to connect with the author.

Denise Sneed Williams

The Tension of Grief

The world was held captive by the news reports, nervously listening to the seemingly overeager reporting of the number of people who had died. It was, perhaps, the first time the playing field had been leveled. Everyone was concerned about this invisible pandemic virus. It was not relegated to age, race, neighborhood, or economics. I would watch the news and pray for the souls of folks and the families of those that I did not know. It felt as if everyone was moving with great tentativeness.

The pandemic shifted everything, including the way we were allowed to lay a person's body to rest. How people were buried was as debilitating as the death itself. The cause did not matter as it was the same protocol. Sometimes, no more than two people were allowed at the gravesite. Sometimes, no flowers were allowed. A lot more cremations were held. A great sense of uncertainty lingered over us. Many are still struggling. I know this because I talk to them, and I am one of them.

Then, I began to experience what I had been praying about in my intimate space. The phone rang, my cousin said, "Aunt Gladys just died."

I hadn't seen my father in three weeks because I had body chills and feared that whatever it was might cause harm to my elderly parents. I would go to the store, clean everything, and take the purchases, which always included flowers, to their house—place them on the porch and step down on the sidewalk as to not transfer anything. One Sunday morning, while picking up the bags, my mother asked if I wanted to come in; I responded, "I do, but I don't know what is wrong with me, and I don't want either of you to get sick." My dad was a larger-than-life man who had become bedridden and had vocal cord paralysis. This was during the time when patients had to be dropped off at the hospital door with no visitors. How would he communicate with the doctors, even though he didn't have the virus? A week later, I was awakened by the phone ringing at 4 a.m. My mother said, "He's gone!" I asked, "Who's gone?" She said, "Your Daddy." My heart was beating so hard, I had to sit for a moment before I threw on clothes to drive to my parents' house."

A few months afterward, I received a text message that a former romantic partner had three weeks to live. Although estranged, I was frantic about speaking to him to settle the differences. While waiting for someone to connect me with him, I received a text, "He's gone."

Six months later, the phone rang with news that my friend Mark was in the hospital. I called him and said, "Baby, what's going on?" Listening to his labored breathing, I asked if he could respond to a text. "Mark, what's happening?" "Pray. Baby, just pray," he said. That was the last time I heard the voice of someone I spoke to nearly every morning. A few days later, he transitioned.

Seven months later, Aunt Retha passed. Six weeks afterward, in the same period between my father and his sister's passing, my sister called to say, "Mama just called and said she needed help." I jumped in my car, not pausing for the lights to change. I ran up the steps to see my sister administering CPR. I held my mom's feet and prayed. My nephew looked on. Even her dog was peering from under the bed in fear.

With only one person allowed to stay at the hospital, we took turns, namely those who didn't live in St. Louis. My son was with my mother when she peacefully transitioned three days later, four days before her 91st birthday. At that moment, I reflected on our last call at 6:00 p.m. Before hanging up, I said, "I love you." She said, "I love you too, Baby." There were no indicators that this would be the last conversation and the last time I would hear my mother's voice.

Several more friends/acquaintances and friends had to say goodbye to their parents. I have helped pen far too many obituaries, and it was all too much! These types of exchanges happened for three years, a total of 12 people who hold heart space.

In the midst, the calls come that say, "I understand exactly how you feel." Yet no one knows how another feels. The experiences might have kinship, but the emotions are intimate, and even with the word capacity as vast as an ocean, no one can transfer the feeling.

Grief is an emotion that commands respect! It does not schedule an appointment, share an agenda, or determine the time to block on your calendar. It just arrives.

According to Webster, tension is the act or action of stretching or the degree of being stretched to stiffness, either by two balancing forces causing or tending to cause extension.

The balancing force for me is knowing that anyone entering the earthly realm shall transition to the next space we cannot see. We trust that what we have read is real. But, and I do mean but, our human emotions beg to be allowed freedom of expression as well. What a dichotomy... knowing and needing.

There are numerous grief counselors and grief circles, of which I chose not to attend either. It's not that I could not benefit from the release; I don't have the capacity to sit in a space with others who might process differently while attempting to manage my own emotions. My cup is perhaps one-half full. This means I have nothing to offer as you pour from the overflow in your saucer, not your cup. If that expression is too much to comprehend, reflect on the instructions given when you get on the plane, not sometimes, every time: "Should there be turbulence and the oxygen mask drops, please put it on yourself before attempting to assist anyone else, including your child." Because humans are who we are, this bit of instruction is given to every passenger, no matter how many flying points you have.

Grief is a process. Initially, in the life celebration/funeral planning stages, the busyness does not allow time to sit with it. But after the ceremonies, the repasts, and all the visitors have gone home, the silence can be so loud that it almost screams. We eagerly celebrate a life's entrance yet have not trained our minds to share the same level of celebration when that soul leaves our presence.

Grief is an emotion that ensures you have loved and have been loved. It is said that grief is like a memory muscle. While the physical presence is gone, the thoughts remain, and subconsciously, you'll look for them. Other times, while moving through your day, a cardinal or a butterfly will land on a bush in your view, or the wind will caress you ever so lightly, or there is a glimpse of a person or a line in a movie, or a song on the radio, or a similar car, or a familiar smile, or deep-set eyes, a sniff of a fragrance, or a seat in their favorite restaurant, or you overhear someone ordering the same complicated coffee concoction or adult beverage, or a word choice string that stops you in your tracks and causes you to inhale, deeply. Then you remember you must exhale. Breathe.

Several years ago, two friends were grieving their mothers; as mine was alive, I had nothing to offer. I could have easily shared scripture, but that was not what they were looking for. Another friend whose mom had also transitioned was at the party. I made the introduction and asked her to speak with them. One said, "They told me it would get better; when?"

Her response was, "It does not get better. You get better." I was down-loading that approach, not knowing that I would have to use those words as a healing balm in the near future, as nothing will ever fill the voids. This level of transition reminded me to share what's on my mind and what I feel because I have no idea if my last conversation with someone will be the last time we speak or if our last visit will be the last visit.

Living with grief reminded me that everything is not serious. I reflected on when I was fighting for my own life and praying for God to heal me. I noted that a large percentage of what I allow mental or emotional space now was unimportant. I concluded that if it was not important when I did not know if I would live, it is not important.

I recognized that too much is taken for granted. In the blink of an eye or a minute later, your entire world could shift without any warning. Not that I was challenged with this before, but I make sure I say what I need to say.

All of us will experience the journey of the physical being separated from the earthly realm. It's an unavoidable life path.

I am reading a book, "The Regrets of the Dying." It is not about dying; it is, however, about the regrets of those who were at the end of their lives and considerations so you may control your own regrets.

My suggestions for living with grief are to pray, be as kind as you can, extend grace to others as well as yourself, embrace the memories, and know that this is a season.

Often, when I talk to people, including close friends, they say, "Denise, you've changed."

I imagine I have.

Denise Sneed Williams has garnered national acclaim and is regarded as an energy shifter. As a speaker, her compelling presentations are sure to cause you to re-evaluate your approach to life with a healthy blend of passionate truth, humor, courage, and heartfelt love, all laced with mother-wit.

As an author, her books have reached audiences worldwide, offering guidance and wisdom on understanding and navigating life's challenges with unwavering grace. She is revered as a trusted advisor—providing individuals empowerment to embrace a holistic approach through faith on their journey to wholeness.

An 11-year breast cancer overcomer, Denise has touched the lives of countless individuals, inspiring hope, healing and transformation. She is extremely vocal about the health care disparities of Black women and knows there is an effective and immediate way to assist those who are often left behind. Denise believes one of the solutions is to marry traditional and holistic medicine, wherein the cause of disease is the focus.

Denise subscribes to 'Empowered women empower women."

She is the mother of three adult children.

Please scan this QR code to connect with the author.

Ly Syin Lobster

Ain't I a Woman?

During college, I pondered," Ain't I a woman?" I understood I was a Black female and cisgender, but as a black female, I struggled with my identity. Which attributes do I subscribe to first, being black or being female? Then, where did Christianity fit in? Reading Bell Hooks' book, "Ain't I A Woman," reminded me of Sojourner Truth's *speech, "Ain't I a Woman,"* at the Ohio Women's Rights Convention in 1851. The social constructs of race and slavery had attempted to strip her of her identity. Despite the social constructs that were believed during her time, Truth thought.

God made her fearfully and wonderfully.

As a Black female in the 21st century, society constantly asks which attribute I identify with first. Is my loyalty to my race or gender? Am I a feminist or womanist? Truth's speech is a great example of why wisdom is referenced as a female pronoun. After reading her iconic speech, I was blown away. I felt proud to be a Black woman. Sojourner Truth was an abolitionist and women's rights activist. Despite her lack of formal education, Sojourner was an intelligent advocate for herself and her people. She was an eminent catalyst for change, and her impact is still felt centuries later. Truth's narrative has confirmed that being passionate about women's issues and Christianity is okay.

I believe the Sojourner Truth statement, "If one woman could turn the world upside down, then a couple of us together can turn it right side up." So, I applied to be the Dress for Success Midwest Community Action Project leader in 2010. After being selected as the leader, I began to research the status of Women in Missouri; the statistics reignited my desire to advocate for women after organizing my fellow Midwest Professional women's group members to provide meals and hygiene products for unhoused women and their families in St. Charles County and the City of St. Louis. We ended the community action project by hosting the "YES WE CAN Women Overcoming Obstacles "conference for unhoused women. The conference concluded with a panel of formerly unhoused women sharing their experiences and wagering the women to look for opportunities to change their situation. I spent the next decade helping women entrepreneurs and nonprofits founded by women and women-led ministries, trying to improve the quality of life for women.

Truth inspires me to be an advocate. She advocated for what she felt was just the treatment of women and African Americans. Since high school, I have known I wanted to be a catalyst for change. Reading an article in the St. Louis Post Dispatch led to my interest in print journalism. I wanted to change the narrative; I didn't like how the media portrayed African Americans.

Sojourner Truth walked away from slavery. Like Truth, I walked away from the bondage of abuse. Similar to Sojourner, I was born into a traumatic environment. My childhood had groomed me for abuse. As a toddler, I was exposed to verbal abuse and patterned the behavior I had observed. While I was in elementary school, I would sit on the back staircase listening to my adult cousin verbally and physically abuse his wife. As an adult, I became involved in abusive relationships. I was not a doormat.

I responded to the abuse by being verbally and physically abusive to my significant others and my children.

While I was working at church, a senior staff member said in a meeting I seemed like an abused woman. That prompted me to seek healing. I had been to counseling and shared about the abuse in my life, but I didn't focus on healing. After attending a support group for domestic and sexual assault survivors, I was inspired to organize and host a domestic violence conference. I used my knowledge from organizing the conference for unhoused women to organize and host a domestic violence awareness event.

Similar to Sojourner, I had some epiphany in my life. My first was that I needed to learn more about spirituality to continue to stay sober. I realized this after several years of sobriety. The next epiphany that changed my life was my last abusive relationship. Domestic violence experts say it takes seven times for a person to leave. I believe it's true. One day, after meeting with a job coach who refused to help until I got out of the abusive relationship, I knew I was just existing and not thriving. But I thought, what if I got into with my partner and I got scared and I hurt him or killed him? I had never thought about that before. In all my abusive relationships, I had been like if I die, I die. I realized at that moment continuing in an abusive relationship was like drinking for me when I had quit. I had a lot of "not yets." I had not yet been shot or stabbed or suffered from being beaten so severely that I had to be hospitalized. I also realized that my response to abuse could lead to prison, death, or life-changing harm. Sojourner was known for sharing her experience with oppression as an enslaved person. I have shared my experience with abuse through blogging and on social media sites. I have participated in domestic violence survivor events and shared my story on various platforms. In 2022, I was a part of a virtual domestic violence town hall hosted by a Missouri State Senator.

Truth has taught me to continue faith in God and eagerly study God's word. Sojourner shared openly about her faith. I started a podcast titled "Stumbling through Christianity," where I learned what I learned from reading the bible, church, and Christian books. That was my way of encouraging others to believe in Christianity. I have tried encouraging others in Christianity by sharing copies of Bruce Wilkinson's book, "The Prayer of Jabez." I believe the prayer of Jabez could have helped Sojourner endure the hardships of slavery, racism, and sexism. Jabez's name meant "great pain." Both Sojourner and I have experienced great pain in our lifetime; we both believe God could expand our territory. We have sought God's protection in traumatic situations. My faith comforted me and empowered me to be resilient despite experiencing abuse, chronic home-lessness, and racial trauma.

Ly Syin Lobster is resilient and resourceful. She was featured as a contributing author in the Intention anthology of the G.R.I.T. series. She is an executive assistant at a local nonprofit in St. Louis, MO, focused on community development. She is a second-generation St. Louisan. She is the mother of two adult children; they are her inspiration and joy.

She has worked with numerous nonprofits, ministries, and small businesses. Ly Syin has been instrumental in empowering women in business, ministry, and nonprofits through Ladies of Inspiration Success. She has also volunteered with organizations such as Ferguson 1000, which, after a successful pilot, expanded into Global 1000. Ly Syin's passion for helping people helps her believe in the concept of investing in people.

She has received recognition twice from the Missouri House of Representatives for remarkable citizenship.

Please scan this QR code to connect with the author.

Angela Lewis

The Power to Heal

I am grateful for the opportunity to share a snippet of my childhood with the hope of inspiring healing in others. Despite the challenges I have faced due to a painful past, I want to emphasize that with God's help, we all have the power inside of us to heal.

As I was growing up, I experienced a lot of verbal abuse in an environment where I was supposed to feel safe. The consistent messages that I was worthless and destined for failure stayed with me despite my efforts to show otherwise. The abuse continued without pause, leading me to develop a strong belief in my inadequacy. I tried my best to make my mother happy, but it never seemed to be enough. As a result, I became a people-pleaser with no sense of my self-worth or esteem, constantly seeking validation.

The slight age gap between my siblings and me only compounded my isolation, driving me to create imaginary companions for solace. It was within this aloneness that my creativity first began to flourish; however, it was a bittersweet reminder of the lack of love and attention I desperately craved.

Opening up about my past has been difficult for me, especially knowing that some of my siblings may not fully grasp the hardships my oldest sister and I endured. It's a part of my childhood that I've always struggled to talk about openly.

I am feeling very anxious about sharing my story, as I know my siblings will never truly understand the pain I went through. The fear of facing their judgment kept me silent, robbing me of showing others that healing is possible. Despite my fears of judgment, I am learning to embrace vulnerability to offer hope to others struggling.

I attempted to share my story with a friend a while back, only to receive a dismissive response: "Well, at least you weren't physically abused like some people are," she said. In that moment, I felt like my emotions were being invalidated and started to believe that maybe I was overreacting. Instead of being supportive, she insinuated that I should be grateful for my situation because it could have been worse. Now, I realize that my experiences are valid and deserving of acknowledgment. I no longer doubt the significance of my emotions and will not diminish my struggles in comparison to others.

School was easy for me, especially in elementary and middle school, because I was successful academically. I thought that if I worked hard enough, I would finally receive the love and acceptance I longed for. Sadly, the abuse never stopped, no matter how well I did. This made me lose all motivation when I started high school. I could not bring myself to the same level of excellence because it seemed like my past accomplishments meant nothing.

In high school, I discovered the art of masking my insecurities and suppressing my emotions. I became so skilled at it that I often felt like I was living a double life, pretending to be someone I was not just to fit in. It is disheartening to think about how much energy I wasted trying to be something I was not, all to avoid facing my true self.

Navigating high school while feeling insecure was challenging, but dealing with it as an adult in the workplace was even more difficult. However, I found a source of hope in the workplace. I was introduced to influential women who took me under their wing, providing mentorship and guidance. I am grateful for all the support they offered for my success. However, I must acknowledge that during that time, I allowed my past trauma to hinder me from achieving my goals.

Despite obtaining a bachelor's degree and writing a book while raising two small children as a single parent, my insecurities weighed heavily on me. Even after proving my mother wrong and earning another degree, I still lacked the confidence I had hoped those achievements would provide.

While I appeared confident and self-assured on the outside, inside, I was experiencing fear and anxiety about things such as making simple decisions, accepting opportunities, and taking risks that could have led to even more opportunities.

I have described the challenges I have encountered with school and work, and I am ready to address the difficulties I faced in relationships. The lack of love drove me to seek it in unhealthy places, resulting in toxic relationships that had a detrimental impact on my self-esteem. It was a struggle to find a relationship where unconditional love was mutual. I consistently gave my all and invested heavily in the other person, often neglecting my own well-being.

My insecurities, low self-esteem, and self-doubt also had a significant impact on my decision-making in relationships. Those negative feelings made me desperate, causing me to ignore warning signs or red flags. As a result, I found myself in an unhealthy marriage where I endured verbal, emotional, and psychological abuse, infidelity, and betrayal because I failed to love myself, acknowledge my self-worth, and lacked the courage to leave.

This chapter only scratches the surface of the trials and tribulations I endured, and it would be a disservice to end the story here. Those who know me understand that I am a Christian who passionately believes in the word of God.

You may wonder, "Where was God in all of this?" That is a great question, and I am grateful you asked. I, too, have questioned God's presence during the abuse I endured.

As new believers, it is natural to question God's whereabouts. However, I believe, as a seasoned saint, it is spiritually immature to think just because you are experiencing hardships that God is not present. The Bible reassures us in Hebrews 13:5 that God will never leave or forsake us, and in Deuteronomy 31:6-8, we are reminded to be strong and courageous, for the Lord our God is with us always.

God never promised us a perfect life, but we can take comfort in the words of Isaiah 54:17. It says, "No weapon formed against you shall prosper, and every tongue which rises against you in judgment you shall condemn." This verse reminds us that although challenges may arise, God is always by our side, promising us victory. I am grateful for this powerful message of faith and protection.

At the beginning of this chapter, I emphasized that we all possess the necessary tools for healing. I have also discussed God's nature and some of his promises to us. You may wonder, "But how do I achieve healing?" My response is simple: TRUST GOD. Trusting God requires faith; however, the Bible teaches us that faith without works is dead.

So, what does trusting God entail? When we trust God, we release all worries and doubts, allowing him to work on our behalf. Nevertheless, it is crucial to understand that trust is only part of the process; we must be accountable for our healing journey. We must also get to know God by immersing ourselves in his word. By applying biblical principles to our lives and spending quality time with God, our trust in him will undoubtedly grow. Additionally, consistent communication with God through prayer is essential for nurturing a deep relationship with him. Lastly, incorporating fasting into our spiritual practice enables us to hear God clearly, exercise self-discipline, and access the power needed to overcome obstacles.

I am grateful to say that I am on the journey towards healing today. I understand that healing is a gradual process, much like any other aspect of life. Just as when you wake up in the morning, you do not just jump out of bed and rush out the door. Most people take the time to brush their teeth, enjoy coffee, shower, and then get ready for the day ahead. Similarly, when seeking employment, you must complete applications, attend interviews, and, with luck, secure a job. The same principle applies to healing - it requires a process.

I am fully committed to doing the necessary work to heal completely, and I am thankful for the support of those who have assisted me on my journey. I want to remind you that you, too, have the power to heal as long as you are determined. With God's help, a positive mindset, and a strong support system, we can overcome any challenge.

I wish you all the best on your healing journey, and may God bless you every step of the way.

Angela Lewis, also known as Author Angela DeMarie, is a native of St. Louis and a talented poet and writer of fiction novels, skits, and plays. Angela's impressive catalog includes two novels, *"Time Doesn't Heal All Wounds"* and *"Time Still Doesn't Heal All Wounds,"* two skits, *"Holy-wood"* and *"The Wrestling Match,"* four plays: *"He Who Is Without Sin," "Our King Has Risen," "What's Good for the Goose"* and *"What Are You Masking?"*

Although relatively new to acting, Angela's portrayal of Beneatha in *"A Raisin in the Sun"* showcases her natural talent and versatility.

Her latest play, *"What Are You Masking?"* delves into low self-esteem, guilt, shame, and anger, with each character finding solace in a closer relationship with God and ultimately celebrating victory over their pain. Angela's ability to craft compelling narratives and meaningful characters sets her apart as a talented and dynamic creative force.

When asked about her passion for writing, Angela explains, "It allows my mind to roam freely without limitations. There are no rules, and I am in complete control."

Please scan this QR code to connect with the author.

Jaime Mowers

A Legacy of Love: Turning the Unthinkable Into the Unstoppable

The bravest thing I've ever done was choose to keep living when I wanted to die.

My life has a permanent line separating the before and after. June 29, 2014, marks that divide. That Sunday, my heart was shattered beyond recognition—beyond comprehension. My dad, Gary A. Baranyai—a loving father and devoted husband, a man with a wide smile and an unforgettable laugh, a kind soul who never knew a stranger, a proud Marine who loved to skydive, my hero, and my best friend—was killed. He was ambushed and murdered—in my house—by my mom's twin sister, who had been like a second mom to me for most of my life.

I still struggle to live in that reality.

My charmed life was instantly obliterated. There was no airbag to cushion the blow, no oxygen mask that dropped down when the news literally took my breath away. It felt like an out-of-body experience as I watched my life splinter into a million pieces. It was hell on earth, yet somehow I was still alive.

The world was no longer the bright, beautiful place I believed it to be. Without my dad's love, light, and over-the-top laughter—and with his killer still alive—the world became dark, disorientating, and terrifying.

My dad and I shared an incredibly special bond. I was always the ultimate "Daddy's Girl." He called me his "Little Girly Whirly." No matter how bad anything seemed, a talk and a hug from my dad always made everything better. Losing him would have been the most difficult thing I ever faced, even under less tragic circumstances. But to lose him in this cruel, horrific way was—and still is—unimaginable, unconscionable.

In the wake of my dad's murder, it wasn't just the complicated, traumatic grief that was all-consuming. My husband and I had to find a new home. My aunt continued to be a terrifying presence in our lives from behind bars. Even now, ten years later, she sometimes still is.

I was consumed by pain, panic, post-traumatic stress disorder, depression, disbelief, and layer upon layer of grief and trauma. I didn't think it was possible to survive the soul-shattering pain. Even if it was, I didn't want to. I was certain I would die of a broken heart, and I welcomed it.

Living in a blur of terrifying days that only continued to get more horrifying, I could see no path ahead or brighter days on the horizon. There's no manual for what to do or how to cope when someone you once loved and trusted takes the life of the person you can't imagine living without.

Everywhere I turned, emotional landmines threatened my very existence. Every time I found the slightest bit of footing, an explosion sent me reeling further into the dark. But I didn't resign myself to staying there.

The greatest lesson my dad taught me was to never, ever give up. As I worked my way through the grief, I promised him I wouldn't. So, I decided I had to keep going until this killed me, and I would fight like hell until it did.

It took grit, courage, perseverance, and strength from my dad and those around me to survive. More than anything, it took a lot of love— an "Army of Love," in fact.

On the first anniversary of my dad's death, my best friends and husband created a Facebook group, invited others, and asked everyone to practice a "Good Deed For Gary" as a way to ease the pain of what would be a difficult day. They even created a hashtag for the occasion—#buzzingloveforgarybee, since shortened to #buzzinglove—because of the "B" initial in my dad's last name and the fun, silly bumblebee gifts he and I often exchanged.

When the day arrived, with the surprise of countless acts of kindness in honor of my dad, I couldn't believe it. I've never been so overwhelmed with love or gratitude. Across the country, friends and strangers brightened their corners of the world. People baked cookies for first responders, helped neighbors, wrote thank you notes to teachers, taped extra dollars to vending machines, overtipped waiters, donated to nonprofits, and much more. It was incredible. Buzzing Love Day became a tradition. It's now a movement.

You never know what someone is going through or how much your kindness could help them. Those small acts of kindness can make a big difference—not just in someone's day, but in someone's life. I know because that's what it did for me. Buzzing Love Day every June 29—and all that Buzzing Love has since become—helped save my life.

This "Army of Love" taught me how to keep living and loving within the pain. Even in the most devastating circumstances, I discovered love, kindness, and beauty in the brokenness. When the pain shattered me, love and kindness saved me.

No one saved me more than my amazing husband and my incredible tribe of best friends, along with strangers who became like family. I am forever grateful to those who saw me in the dark, grabbed their flashlights, and shined their light in my face.

My husband reminded me that I had everything I needed within me to keep going. He told me to look at our precious Pomeranians, Foxy and Bear-Bear, and said, "The boys and I need you." I replayed that moment in my head countless times. It became my life preserver.

I recalled the time when my dad saw me struggling to finish a marathon. He jumped in—literally—from the sidelines, running beside me in jeans and cheap tennis shoes for the final six miles. He chanted Marine Corps anthems, and we talked about how Baranyais never give up. We crossed the finish line holding hands, arms above our heads, all smiles.

When I told my therapist I didn't know how I was going to get through this, she said, "You are doing it." On one of my hardest days, my best friend said, "It will not always be this way." Those words—the possibility that it might not always be this painful or would at least be livable at some point—gave me hope.

Sometimes, believing in the potential is the best we can do. At the time of my dad's murder, I was in the middle of training for an Ironman triathlon. During the weeks and months preparing for the 2.4-mile swim, 112-mile bike ride, and 26.2-mile run, I suspended my doubts about whether I could accomplish the 140.6-mile feat. Exactly eight weeks after my dad was killed, I crossed the finish line at Ironman Louisville, achieving what I once thought impossible. This helped me believe I might somehow be able to get through the unthinkable of losing my dad.

Was I strong enough when I started training? No. But I built strength along the way, despite navigating immense grief. Building physical endurance helped me endure the mental anguish, anxiety, and depression, and when race day arrived, I was strong enough.

In much the same way, I built strength and resilience each day I survived without my dad. Nearly three years after he was murdered,

I gathered all of the courage I had and faced his killer in court. Being a voice for my dad—and finding my own again—helped me reclaim my life. I became the strongest version of myself and truly started living again. I became unstoppable.

I'm grateful I kept going, even when I didn't think it was possible to withstand the pain. I would have missed out on so much life. I became an Ironman. I found unexpected healing among a herd of bison in Yellowstone National Park. I discovered some peace standing on the precipice of vast canyons that made my pain feel smaller, more distant, and less consuming. I laughed and smiled again. I became an owner of my hometown newspaper. I've shared Buzzing Love with thousands of people.

My husband and I added two precious Pomeranians to our original two-pom pack of love and fluff. We've had amazing adventures, met the best of friends, and cherish the sweet, simple moments. His love carried me through the hours and days I didn't think I could survive, helping heal the hurt in a way that only he could. He keeps my dad's love and laughter alive while keeping me grounded in the here and now, focusing on the joy.

I wouldn't have made it to today without the love, support, and friendship of the strong and amazing women surrounding me, including my mom. My parents' unconditional love and encouragement made me who I am. In my dad's absence, my mom's love has continued to overflow, spilling into the cracks of my heart that most need healing.

There are still many difficult days when I remind myself that it won't always be this way. I also remind myself that at any given moment, we have the power to say, "This is not how my story ends." Life will require you to be braver than you could ever imagine. You'll be exhausted, scarred, and bruised, but eventually, it will be possible to smile, laugh, and feel joy again.

More than ten years later, I'm still learning to navigate this loss and all of the other losses that came with it. I've worked hard at my recovery. I've learned that grief and pain never go away, but they evolve. Grief changes shape, size, texture, ebbs and flows, and varies in intensity. There is no way around it — only continually through. You absorb it and learn to carry it. For as much as it hurts, it's possible to channel much of that pain into love. And hopefully, somewhere along the way, you can use it to help bring a little healing into someone else's heart.

In loving memory of Gary A. Baranyai — Best Dad Ever.

Jaime Mowers is a Webster Groves native and graduated from Webster Groves High School in 2000. After graduating from Southwest Missouri State University (now Missouri State University) with a journalism degree in 2004, she worked as a reporter at the *Rolla Daily News*, *Springfield News-Leader*, and *Sullivan Journal.*

Mowers became a reporter at the Webster-Kirkwood Times when she and her husband moved back to St. Louis in 2011. She became an owner and editor-in-chief of the Times in September 2020 when she and longtime employees Randy Drilingas and Kent Tentschert purchased the paper from former publisher Dwight Bitikofer, reviving the paper after a hiatus in printing due to the pandemic.

Mowers is the founder of Buzzing Love, a kindness project founded in memory of her dad, Gary Baranyai. She is also a triathlete and lives in Maplewood with her husband, Travis, and their three Pomeranians: Bear-Bear, Mr. Puffers, and Teddy.

Please scan this QR code to connect with the author.

Connie Ninfa Mayta

The Story of My Power and *Mi Sabiduria*

My wise grandfather said, *"La persona que lo quiere, lo hace."* The person who really wants it will act on it. (Guadalupe Saenz, RIP).

With that inspiration, I have set the course to write in this anthology to honor my ancestors and empower others. I am fueled by the Holy Spirit, who is always with me, invoked or not.

I will display this quest with my past, present, and future so the reader will know how I got here, where I am now, and my vision for the future. No matter how many decades we have experienced, I believe today is an awesome day to design the rest of our lives with intentionality.

Power & *Sabiduria* from my Past

How did I get here? I was born in Altus, Oklahoma. A field on my birth certificate reads: "Occupation of Parent: Cotton Picker." My Texan parents were both born in the Rio Grande Valley, worked in the fields, and migrated to various harvest locations within the United States. In a sense, we were yanked by caravanning to harvest-ready crops. Our housing consisted of camp casitas, rented multi-family houses, and various shared living quarters. My grandfather led the way as he knew the way of the farmers.

Mom's photos of us in this *campo* life showed us smiling, happy as little larks. Were these masks? When I was seven, my dad was offered a permanent job in Michigan, which was on our migrant route. We settled in Holland, Michigan, "Where it's Tulip Time in May," and where it is miserably cold in February, our move month.

My father was like our Moses, and we were the children who could not understand why my dad took us out of the migrant stream. Why would anyone disrupt our golden years? I did not understand as a child that both my parents were among the eldest and had their education stolen when they were yanked out of school and yanked into fields. Their hands and backs pulled weeds, harvested, and toiled so their younger siblings and we could have better lives.

My parents are the heroes of my early era. After having four kids, they both achieved their GEDs in Michigan. My father became a maintenance journeyman, and my mom eventually obtained her Bachelor's and Master's Degrees in Bi-Lingual Teaching. That takes and gives great faith, and I am forever indebted to Luciano Hernandez Azuara and Eva Saenz Hernandez.

Thus, my formative years were in this quaint Dutch-American settlement, where I found friends and found my strengths. My best friends were Dutch Christian Reformed gals whom I Dutch Danced with—happily in wooden shoes while donning at least 13 pairs of socks. Did my golden years shift to this timeframe? Or were they still to come?

I started going for what I designed for myself and noticed people asking me, "Where's the fire?" My propelling drive has been to honor my grandparents, who created jobs for many families on the migrant agricultural caravans. Yes, there's leadership in the migrant stream. Many of my aunts and uncles fought for the rights of migrant workers so that we may have a better life. Their acts included marching with Cesar Chavez, participating in *juelgas*, and creating examples of how education will afford us choices. I was on a mission because of them! Still am!

In my middle era, I lost all four grandparents; may they rest in Heavenly Peace. They taught my parents to raise us while keeping our traditions. There was always faith, music, and dancing, like during my beautiful *Quinceanera*. There was a time when it seemed I had a golden touch for what I wanted or saw. If I chose it and named it, I would be determined to make it happen and have a litany of accomplishments in my high school yearbook as a record.

What were my regrets in this era? Nothing. And what would I design for the next era in my life? Stacking up studies, accomplishments, and adventurous travel, I also resolved to get married to someone so that I could live happily ever after.

Power & *Sabiduria* in My Present

The present is relative to leaving my formative years and blending into the day when I woke up this morning.

The golden touch waned. I started to experience life choices, not getting what I chose. I changed college studies and married later in life, derailing my plans. I suffered and created my own great depression. It seemed ironic that the litany of scholarly accomplishments, adventurous travel, and making a decent corporate living in my strengths, had begotten me a depressive life.

For over 15 years, I was stuck in my rut, and I shamefully blamed others. Eventually pivoting, I started meeting people who inspired me beyond my immediate family. My colleagues and faith mates helped me understand that true happiness comes from serving others. And I was relieved from depression after dishing out forgiveness to others. I dusted off my band flute, joined the choir, and expanded various ministries. I bless my friends and my heroes from God. I would surpass my word allocation if I named them all. Humbling myself and acknowledging the Greater Being is in control of my life.

Then, I continued building my litany of accomplishments in professional work and took on leadership roles in professional organizations. Joining Toastmasters International, the Project Management Institute, and the Maxwell Leadership Team helped me focus on developing others.

This was my pinnacle of making holy moments for others. I grew immensely as a leadership development coach with the Maxwell Leadership Team. This allowed me to serve countries like Paraguay (2016) and Costa Rica (2018). I served in two transformation missions comprising 200 leadership coaches to help these countries develop their aspiring leaders. In each mission week, we planted the leadership seed in 15,000 people. Having a bi-lingual mind and heart, I was able to go into more remote landscapes of these countries where I heard people rise and say, "I know what I must do." Did they realize they were blessing me? I loved empowering the voiceless. Hint: This helps cure depression. What depression?

Continuing in my current golden years, I am now married to Juan Carlos Mayta, and we have a wonderful Aussiedoodle, Breezie. I remember how my parents warned me, "You had better study so that you do not have to work in the fields." Well, my conquistador/agronomist/ husband studied to work in the agricultural fields. Wherever the crops yank us, I accompany my Christian husband serving in our church. I can see clearly now that he is my self-proclaimed "trophy husband" for whom God wanted me to wait. I don't wait well.

The undertone of healed depression has a lot of temptation to succumb to returning to being sad. The evil tempter wants me to despair and worry about what could have been and what about my parents' health in Michigan. However, my supportive friends and coaches have greater strength in their pinky than that evil one who wants to hurl me down. The Lord assured me in my spiritual exercise, *"I will be with you in the hospital rooms and the ballrooms."*

What were my regrets in this era? Giving time to depression while I was learning from my failures. And what would I design for the next period in my life? I am developing a portfolio called "Multiple Streams of Income and Service," building on my strengths and healed scars.

Power & *Sabiduria* For My Future

Having just written these words for my future, I will invoke the Holy Spirit to lead my entrepreneurial endeavors. I am positive this will keep me out of depression. It will not be without its dramatic "plunger tugs" on my heart as I suffer the dismays of my professional life and lose heroes in my life. However, they will forever be present in my heart's imagination. As the song goes, "Memories bring back you." The truths I hold steadfast in my heart will stay because I intentionally hold them there. Thy Word have I hid in my heart... *Psalm 119 (KJV).*

I may not have been able to recognize my bliss today if it had not been for the depression. Did I just express fondness for the D-word? I am very grateful that my humble failures have created streams of service for me as a facilitator, trainer, and coach. The coach that I have become loves the thought of putting a song in your heart to get you through your day, your chapter, or your celebration. I'd love to maximize a connection or bring down a star closer to you, so long as you point to the star you dream of.

Another stream in my service portfolio includes teaching in my strengths. As a portfolio manager, I will be authoring more details of my three ages of life as sampled here. I will tell stories, and when I grow tired or need words, I'll ask AI to help me write. I love that I am experimenting with AI. I feel kind of modern, like I've still got it.

It's actually the Holy Spirit that propels me. All my future, of course, is *"Primero Dios!"* God's Will first. I'll squirm and weep until I can sing, "It Is Well With My Soul."

Power in Education and Professional Organizations:
- Holland Christian High School, Holland, MI
- Bachelor's Science, Engineering Graphics, Kalamazoo, MI
- Master of Science, Management, Project Management, Colorado Springs, CO
- Project Management Institute Professional Certifications:
  - [PMP] Project Management Professional, Minneapolis, MN
  - [PfMP] Portfolio Management Professional, Saint Louis, MO
- Toastmasters International: [DTM] Distinguished Toastmaster, Minneapolis, MN

Wisdom in my Christian Meditation:
I humbly look to my past and would give anything to run around my grand-parents' house with my cousins in the Rio Grande Valley in Texas. At night, we played jacks on their porch and danced. When did this music stop?

In the days between, I studied hard, stumbled hard, and made many friends who have helped me seal my faith. My depressive failures strengthened me so that I could fall forward in God's plan for me, and I am walking in the place that once was God's vision for me.

For my present and future, I'd dedicate myself to being the voice of the voiceless in my communities, using my strengths in leading people, facilitating projects, and coaching to glorify my Lord.

Please scan this QR code to connect with the author.

Nicci Roach

...and then I saw her

"You've always had the power, my dear;
you just had to learn it for yourself."
– Glinda from The Wizard of Oz

A few years back, life was flourishing for this middle-aged woman. She was a commanding presence, a Black woman who drew attention when she stepped into a room. Decorated with many credentials and accolades, she captivated hearts with boundless generosity. Her very essence left a seductive vibration and, at other times, a lingering sweet fragrance that filled the spaces she appeared, a testament to her grace and impact. It was evident that her words and actions were infused with activated faith. Doors were swinging open, inviting her into new realms of experience and opportunity. Her reputation birthed a personal tagline suggesting she was a leader's leader. Yet, in this celebrated existence, suddenly, she found herself unprepared for what life had to offer—entry into a dry place.

What is this dry place? A place where there is a pace of progress, but you feel stuck. It is a place of service, but self-worth is interrogated—a place where there is an abundance of imagination but resistance to execution. Being surrounded by people, even ones you love, but grieving the absence of connection—a place where you see the manifestation of your prayers but fear clutching and walking in the provision. A place where you're in the posture of praise, but the promises of God seem inaccessible. While this place offers a subtle yet luring invitation, there's sure inner conflict happening within this isolated bubble.

But can a person who has access to so much and is celebrated by so many enter a dry place? Is this even possible?

Well, she did and eventually spiraled down a path of self-sabotage while sipping on a mocktail of insecurity, self-deprecation, fear, doubt, and imposter syndrome. She was marinating in the idea that maybe she needed to turn her life volume down, supposing living too loud was not pleasing to God and could make others uncomfortable. It's funny how some folks agreed. They encouraged her to find balance to lower her levels, suggesting it didn't take all that. That's because they were living their best life on low and some on mute. She agreed to such foolishness that caused her to compromise matters of the heart and her divine calling.

She even found herself attempting to resurrect things of old while celebrating shallow victories, past accomplishments that once fed the ego but were no longer relevant. Although she was humble, the ego yearned to be satisfied. This tug-of-war prevented her from seeing the bigger picture, the next phase of her journey, attempting to emerge like a tulip from the earth in early spring in its proper season.

I deliberately slowed down to engage and check in on her. To my surprise, it wasn't the cloth face mask she wore for the pandemic virus protection that proved challenging to remove. It was the invisible mask she wore that posed the real obstacle. This invisible mask concealed a host of true feelings, fears, intentions, vulnerabilities, insecurities, pain, dreams, and more. It even concealed her fear of success and her hesitation to accept an opportunity she had prayed for.

After some tough conversations with her, slowly, after more than 365 days of sheltering in place, she began to peel off that invisible disguise. To her surprise, layers needed to be pulled away. She realized the mask was an obstruction to purpose and no good for her well-being. Finally surrendering to a Psalm 23 experience, the stilled waters provoked reflection and restoration from that dry place.

You may ask, why do I know so much about this woman's story? Why was I so invested? Well, my urgent intrusion into her world is because I am HER! Yes, she is me.

Once the layers of that invisible mask were removed, I witnessed my reemergence, and it took my breath away. I exposed my full, true, imperfect, yet authentic self - inside and out. I discovered that I already possessed everything I needed for success, but I had to define it for myself.

You should see me now, draped in confidence, empowered, and dressed in the whole armor. My smile is magnetic, radiating from the depths of my being. The way I move often halts bystanders in their tracks. It is my sure surrender that guides me, fortifies me, and prompts me to seek support when needed. I serve from a place of bounty rather than scarcity. Though I may not possess millions, I meticulously plan moments to uplift others unselfishly. I no longer give weight to others' opinions about me or my manner of contribution - they are merely fleeting perspectives. Accomplishing my goals no longer surprises me, and I anticipate victory because I am prepared for such outcomes. I have ceased trying to blend in, recognizing my voice as a unique input into global exchanges. I have arrived at a place where I wholeheartedly embrace myself, conscious of my existence, a masterpiece, flaws and all.

I remind myself to infuse intention into every word, thought, and action. I encourage myself to intentionally occupy space. I seek out ways to harmonize provocative insights. I remind myself that failing doesn't mean I should abort or abandon but rather assess, activate, and abound. I prompt myself to grant self-benevolence regarding outputs and inputs.

I hint at ways to whisper sweet somethings to my spirit. I consistently confirm my understanding concerning who holds the power and the promises.

I'm tickled at my annoying attempt to add a subtle sway to my every step while displaying confidence parallel to my elders, who always assured me, 'Everything would be alright in the mo(*u*)rning.' I was already familiar with these movements of exodus, but this place, this space, was different, and I needed to be ushered into a self-centered space to reset, regain, and revive. I needed to move with a sense of urgency and an unrepentant stance and not be paralyzed by permissions. I was reminded that goodness and mercy were still following me, and I couldn't separate from either of them even if I tried.

I also recalled the need to BE STILL (and not feel guilty) and KNOW. It was in the stillness that I realized the dry space was, in fact, a season of divine disruption. It was a season to reflect and gain clarity, a season to reduce distractions, a season for healing, honesty, expanded thought, self-rediscovery, amplified vision, and the rethinking of possibilities. I was reminded that I wasn't meant to fit in, and what I doubted most about myself was the very thing people celebrated. It was a time when pain and purpose were happening simultaneously. Now, I felt myself being readied for uncharted, expanded territory.

There would be no more conceding to insecurities and societal pressures or being confined by mediocre standards, and this season warranted a stance of trusting and obeying while disregarding accolades or an attempt at perfection. I realized that the life I once knew was only a fraction, a foretaste of the blessings yet to unfold. No person or thing could carry me through this process. The season of elevation was upon me, but I had to descend before the ascension. I now grasp the necessity for an appointed leader to navigate through such occasions.

As appointed leaders—*individuals who are chosen to lead by way of an assignment, a pivotal responsibility rather than self-selection or election*—we can get so engrossed in our actions that we fail to recognize when the assignment is complete or has reached a natural pause. Understanding the rhythm enables us to serve from a place of purity; not one rattled with internal and external selfish motives, regret, or manipulation.

On the flip side, appointed leaders who don't realize they're wearing a mask and have failed to check in with themselves are sure to burn out, becoming frustrated, if not defeated, by the very assignment that captured our hearts. Yes, even good work can steer us down shadowy paths. Far too many of us appointed leaders are trying to pour from an empty cup. Some from a used cup. We're attempting to influence but stagnant ourselves. We're busy but not producing. We're communicating but not transmitting. We're present, but somehow we've vanished. We're attempting to give what we ourselves honestly don't have and allowing past victories to become our metric for success.

As an appointed leader, over time, we find ourselves operating from an unaligned place and time. If you're not careful, you might find yourself masking your true self, leading to self-doubt and irrelevance. This can result in internal voids, deficient conditions, and emotional and spiritual bankruptcy. These fractured existences yearn for recovery and revival. It's better to reset, regain, and revive along the journey; however, consider divine disruptions that may come to nudge you. Guard against the potential to distract or depress you. Rather, embrace the reality that this is a preparation to launch into the next assignment.

Appointed leaders pour and give from a deep place; however, you can not continue to pour and never refill. Take time to discover what replenishes your spirit and nourishes the depths of your soul. Take the needed time to realign, as often as necessary, unapologetically and without announcement. Be sure to keep your eyes on her; don't let her out of your sight. Check for any masks. Develop her. Turn the volume up for her. Love on her. Pause for her. Then position her to give and receive, for the time has come to possess new land flowing with new promises bearing her name.

> *"For I know the plans I have for you," declares the Lord,*
> *"plans to prosper you and not to harm you,*
> *plans to give you hope and a future."*
> *– Jeremiah 29:11 (NIV)*

Nicci Roach is an educator and curator of clout who excels at considering the whole person or organization. She has a unique talent for diversifying rooms—domestic and international—with equipped leaders through curated educational ecosystems. Her teachings, research, and service facilitate enhanced equity, influence, and leadership.

Nicci has served in various capacities within higher education, making significant contributions towards DEIAB, change management, organizational development, and leadership development. She is the founder of covenant exCHANGE, llc, a trusted partner in learning and development consulting. She also launched CLOUT Inc., a nonprofit research and strategy organization that provides evidence and tactics to support upward mobility, retention, and equity for those from underrepresented populations. Her insights are also shared through radio and television programming.

A lifelong learner, Nicci has completed studies at Webster University, Cornell University, and Harvard University. She is now completing a doctoral dissertation at Missouri Baptist University.

Please scan this QR code to connect with the author.

Jana M. Gamble

Hola mi amor!
Hello, my love!

This is a letter to my younger self. Jana Marie Gamble, we need to talk, Sister. I speak to you with a sense of urgency, so I must go back in time to meet you where we were. Many have said that you should be careful what you ask for. I realize this warning is coming too late in some cases, yet it will benefit you greatly throughout your future.

Baby girl, you have been through so many ups and downs. We've experienced childhood trauma, self-injury, over a decade battling bulimia, and Daddy issues as a child of divorce, cultural identity challenges as a multicultural human from a small town, and the list goes on.

Guess what, though? You're still here! God brought you through every one of those circumstances. You are living again!

Now, mi amor. Never in our history together have we had a moment like this, but guess what? Now is an essential time to share these truths with you. It's imperative that I provide you with the insight you will need to find the will to fight through this next season. It's going to be one of the toughest rides of your life, Jana. But you've got this! Please hear me now; it will not be enough in your own power or strength. Stay with me. Stay focused. Give it everything you have, even when you think you have nothing to give. Remember that you are a child of God, and believe it or not, you are human. This will be your SHIFT to live. This time around, we are going to be healing- On Purpose!

Jana Marie Gamble, I need you to sit down for this one. Better yet, would you like to lay down, amor? Aye, I think that this one calls for an internal recording for sure. You're going to need it. Yo mismo estas listo? Ready? Set. Aqui vamos!

Let me set the stage for you as we begin. After missing your first flight you've just returned from South Africa (SA) just in time for your daughter, Dyawna's, 8th grade graduation. She's still living her best life running track and has qualified for the Junior Olympics (J.O.) again! You're working your side hustle as a banquet server at Marriott to stack extra money for this year's J.O. experience. You're still on a high from the extraordinary mission work and SA adventures.

"Jana. Jana!
Two glazed-over brown eyes open sluggishly with a deep
      Appearance of anguish written all over them.
Lids heavy like concrete fight to tolerate the overtly bright lights.
Feet stumble to and fro with hands desperately looking for
      Stability and to support the frontal lobe.
The room feels cold
Confusion overflows from her cup.

"Hey, are you okay?!

The way He created me, my heart feels for others, so although I can't see straight or hardly contain the pain I'm feeling, I instantaneously choose their feelings above my own.

"Yeah, yeah. I'm okay. I just need a minute."

Feet moving amiss, I drunkenly depart to find a dark, quiet place to park where, Lord willing, no one else is near. As my hand anchors my cabeza, the surface expands with full intentions.

"Jana, are you okay? What happened? Do you need something?"

Um…yeah. Um, I just, uh, need. Actually, can you get me some ice, please? I got hit in the head. She hit me in the head with the… with the coffee cup rack thing.

"Oh my God! Your head! Here's some ice. You should probably go down to see Nurse Abby."

Um…maybe. I definitely need some medicine.

Everything is moving in slow motion but feels like an eternity. Eyes blurry and legs like they're fresh off the sea, I venture unaccompanied to the HR department, where I'm greeted by the nurse with whom I, unfortunately, have had far too many moments throughout my employment at Marriott.

"Hey, what's going on?"

I share how, while making coffee stations with my co-worker, she didn't see where I was before she swung the full coffee cup dishwasher rack from about 6 feet high straight down into the left side of my forehead. We had a chat, I asked for medicine, and I asked to lie down. The next thing I know, I'm out cold.

Hola mi amor. Can you hear me? Don't be alarmed. You can continue to rest; for your sake that will be best at this moment. We need to have a little chat, okay? My eyes are taut, and my screen is black. The only audio is streaming from my voice in full Dolby TrueHD from an unknown location fathomless within me.

I, well yo mismo; let's just go with "we," have arrived at the inception of the darkest, most devastating developmental season of our life. Every single episode will be a test to fight if you'll survive. It will depend on how you respond to every attack and fiery dart thrown at you to whether you will come out of all of this dead or alive. This will determine if you will come out bitter, your heart stone cold, or become who you were created to be, living life on fire with a heart of gold. No matter what happens, who leaves you, or what it may look like financially or even in the natural, you must know that this battle is bigger than you. This war is over your life, your purpose, and the position you are meant to play in the Kingdom. Do not quit! Do not give up! You are and always have been enough!

Let's take a deep breath and dive in, mi amor.

EPISODE 1 | The Mission to Dismiss You

Head constantly pounding like a jackhammer
Nausea so bad like the first trimester
Why does every hair on my head feel so painful
Trying to sleep- tried every angle
They're dismissing my pain I get angered
But it's a setup — that's what they get paid for

EPISODE 2 | Don't Let Her Go, Fight For Her Life

Been fast, like lighting since the Ravens
Indoor meet she's bound for greatness
Wait…she's on the ground now her heat is over
ER Bound, doctors rounds the reports are no good
Kidneys failing, Mami's wailing in the breakroom
Constant prayers, scents and songs in the air of Lauren Daigle

EPISODE 3 | Get Your Knee off My Neck, I CAN'T BREATHE!!!

Window open what ya doing
Hey, why you fakin'
Oh my God I'm frozen, I can't escape it
I know it's the virus!
Lord, how do I have no sense?!
George Floyd's in all the headlines
Running PR from my beside
I CAN'T BREATHE
I think I may die

EPISODE 4 | My Authentic Cries

Symptoms still persistent pain in my chest
Wheelchair-bound no breath to share the rest
PCP says it's in my head
Can't speak — using text to talk instead
Found the Virus Clinic — praise God no wait list
Daily therapies — like a full-time job I'm just trying to exist

EPISODE 5 | ¡El Tiempo de Tu Vida! *The Time of Your Life*

Mobility Scooter y maletas we take flight
Mijita y yo in Mexico for the first time
Finally a chance to actually unwind
Poolside, deep dives, ATVs and a boat ride
Cooking classes, refill our glasses a chance to explore
Cancun it owes us nothing, but we're going back for sure

EPISODE 6 | College Bound:
Breaking the Cycle, Letting Her Soar

Health scares and false evidence appearing real
Father's passed, single Mami no income for years
Learning to trust my seed in God's hands
Endless hours of scholarship apps
And… acceptance into 13 schools, which to choose
Distance is her preference, sprinting is her heart's desire
Unlimited faith this will require

EPISODE 7 | This Means War: Confusion is Not from Him

Strange knocks and feet through my door
Unknown man "representing" the owners saying here we can
Live no more
Constant confusion, do we stay or do we go
Speak, Lord, I truly do not know
Open-house strangers in and about
False hope, disrespect and even more doubt
Moving out

EPISODE 8 | The Time Has Come: Your Healing Springs Forth

Months of invites, morning prayer
Plans to be in His house but migraine bound
Fri-daze turn to FriNays!
My stallion Ace, I'm in love
Birthiversary, Don't Muzzle Me, altar call
Mother Joan he summons to me
Prophecy "Full recovery"
"Can you faith walk for me"
The sound of victory

EPISODE 9 | The Perfect Movement of God: My Resurrection Day

7 weeks on Zoom, new member
Coming in assistance free, a walking miracle
Leading Ace, his warm embrace, don't want this to end
Graduation I'm advancing
My story has just begun
Pastor calls, I give it my all
I'm dancing now, my resurrection!

Entonces mi amor, I see you stirring, but before you wake, there are just a few more words I need to say. To make it to the me that is speaking to thee, it won't be in your own power or your wisdom alone that saves you. It's by the grace of God that you will make it through. Be gentle with yourself. Take one step and breath at a time. God has called you to do great things and—On Purpose He will continue to use you and I. Te amo mucho mi amor.

Jana M. Gamble is a producer, screenwriter, assistant director, speaker, author, and advocate. Her company, Purposed Productions,' mission is to transform hearts and minds around the world through eye-opening dynamic speaker and artist expression, media-focused youth education and empowerment, and healing-centered events.

She joined the Hollywood Prayer Network while fighting the global virus during the dueling pandemics. She heard God's call to take on the Local Chapter Director role for the Hollywood Prayer Network St. Louis, where HPN was birthed 20 years prior.

Jana self-published the books, *"107 Ways to Give When You Think You Have Nothing to Give," "Capture Your Giving and Blessings: A Journaling Journey to a New Discovery," "I Am A Child of God"* and *"Are You Human?"*

Ms. Gamble is the proud mother of Jabri, Dyawna, and Mamba. Jana resides in St. Louis, MO, where she is a member and on staff at The Advancing Church.

Please scan this QR code to connect with the author.

Diane Carson

Turning Setbacks into Success

I have always been someone who looks at the glass half full. At age 10, I was deposited in a British boarding school, in a room filled with 9 strange girls. My parents, like other middle-class British parents, decided that a boarding school education would provide discipline and independence and serve me well as an adult. I remember my parents driving three hours to deliver me to the school in Bideford, North Devon. I had no idea where we were going. Stunned and not knowing where I was or why I was there, I watched my parents' backs as they left the room. I was sitting on a creaky old iron bed with no idea where I was or what I had done to be ripped from my home and everything I knew and loved.

Just as in the movie "Mean Girls," the girls in my dorm room were abusive bullies, each of them fighting to become popular. Looking back on my boarding school experience, I'm convinced my ADHD caused a lot of the trouble that I had fitting in. But I learned to fend for myself in that bleak room filled with 10 cold iron beds and one marble-topped dresser per bed with three drawers to put all our worldly belongings.

As a Navy brat, I had attended 10 schools in 6 years. My education was lacking in several areas, and I was always "the new girl" when I was introduced to the class at each new school. Boarding school was supposed to bring some normalcy and discipline into my life. Instead, I rebelled against all the rules. I was kept back a year because of my inability to focus and follow the rules. I had no idea I would be held back until I was back at the school for the next term. I was shocked, ashamed, and depressed. But instead of rebelling, I used that negative energy to win the Most Improved Student Award for that year!

At 17, the Royal Navy transferred my father to a position in the United States. Because I had just graduated from school, I had no choice but to travel with my parents to St. Louis. I didn't grow up in St. Louis; I didn't go to high school there and was devastated. With eight years of elocution, I earned a scholarship to the Royal Academy of Dramatic Arts, but I had to put it on hold. I looked different, my accent was different, and I had difficulty making friends. But I made the best of it—grew my hair, lost my accent, and tried desperately to fit in.

At 19, when my parents returned to the UK, I married the first guy to pay attention to me. It wasn't until we were married that I found out how narcissistic he was and what a bad temper he had. The fact that he pushed me up against the wall, threw his dinner on the floor when he didn't like it, and always sabotaged my friendships may have been a red flag! However, I stayed with him for 28 years, walking on eggshells, until my 10-year-old son told me he was scared and we needed to leave. Soon after, I was beaten with a fist across my face in front of my son, and my eardrum was injured. That was the last straw. We left in the early morning with just the clothes on our backs and moved in with my husband's brother and his wife. We were scared to death.

By then, I was in my late forties. Within two weeks of receiving my divorce (on Halloween night, I might add!), I was downsized from my corporate job. My position was eliminated. I was a single mother with no relatives or support system. I decided no one was going to do that to me again (I was downsized from my first job at the British Consulate General 18 years prior.) With my background in PR and events, I formed a marketing company with a partner and started to build the company from scratch.

I had a lot of friends who saw me through a difficult time, and I found out how great they were when I suffered a twisted fracture in my leg six months after forming the marketing company with my best friend (or so I thought at that time). I was in a wheelchair for six months, dealing with an angry son because I couldn't take him to visit friends, go to the mall, etc. It was a tough time.

Fast forward to seven years ago when my then-best friend and business partner decided she had had enough; she was quitting and wanted out of our partnership that day. I was devastated, angry, upset, and hurt. We had been business partners for over 20 years with no arguments. I was completely shocked. By then, I was in my mid-60s and not ready to retire, so I formed my own company, Promo Xpertz, specializing in helping clients select just the right creative and budget-friendly items for trade shows and to brand themselves (have to get that ad in there!). I started from scratch, researching networking groups and attending every event I could. I joined organizations, chambers, anywhere I could meet potential clients. Now in my mid-70s, I love what I am doing and having a ball meeting wonderful new people.

My goal is not to network and join organizations to get clients but to build relationships. If business develops, it is a bonus. I am in charge of my destiny and make my own decisions. No matter what hand I have been dealt, I have always taken my power back and used my resilience to reinvent myself.

Why am I telling you all this? My philosophy is never give up on your dreams! When you are knocked down, get back up. Be in charge of your life. Don't let others make decisions on how you should live your life. Behind every cloud, there is a rainbow. Things will always be better, and out of every bad experience, there is always goodness.

Diane Carson is a certified marketing consultant (CMC) and the president/owner of Promo Xpertz LLC. Diane collaborates with small businesses, entrepreneurs, and nonprofits, guiding them to select memorable and useful branded items within their budget. With 8 years at the helm of Promo Xpertz LLC and an additional 15 years as co-owner of a full-service marketing company, she has a wealth of experience creating and implementing effective marketing action plans.

Throughout her career, Diane's strengths have shone through in her organizational and administrative skills, strong motivational abilities, enduring professional relationships, and a commitment to high-quality standards. Diane has been a driving force behind the growth of small businesses and entrepreneurs. Her focus on highly targeted promotional marketing programs and strategic marketing has been instrumental in helping clients to succeed.

Diane continues to bring creativity, dedication, and a strong work ethic to her clients, taking their "Brand Beyond the Bland!"

Please scan this QR code to connect with the author.

Tina Meier

My Daughter Megan: A Life That Sparked Change

After a few long work days, I boarded the plane home to St. Louis, MO. I settled into my seat, fastened my seatbelt, closed my eyes, and took a deep breath. Suddenly, I heard little voices in the seats in front of me. Two young girls were bombarding their mom with questions about how long it would take to see their grandparents at the airport. The mom explained that they would board another plane to Disney World after a couple of hours. The girls' excitement was palpable, and they chatted animatedly about all the fun they would have.

Their joy took me back to when I took my daughters, Megan and Allison, to Disney World. Seeing their eyes light up at the sight of the parades was magical. Tears started streaming down my face as I tried to hold back my sobs. Each breath hurt, and I didn't want to draw attention to myself. If someone asked if I was okay, I wouldn't have been able to answer. The pain was overwhelming, and I turned my head toward the window, trying to hide my tears. I thought to myself, "How did I get here? This wasn't supposed to be my life. I was never supposed to bury my 13-year-old daughter, Megan."

My Background

I was born Christina Marie Greco on July 22, 1970, but I've always gone by Tina. Growing up in St. Charles, Missouri, I was the older of two children. My younger brother Tony, who passed away in 2009, was four years younger than me. My early years were filled with happiness, love, and laughter but also sadness and grief.

My father, Larry Greco, passed away from a brain tumor when I was only fifteen. His death was hard on me, and I mentally checked out through most of high school. Despite this, I graduated in 1988 and got married at 19 years old.

My first daughter, Megan Taylor Meier, was born November 6, 1992. Holding her for the first time, I was overwhelmed by my love for her. She had two huge dimples, bright, sparkling eyes, and brown curly hair. She was the most beautiful child I had ever seen.

On May 31, 1996, Allison Paige Meier was born. Another gorgeous baby girl with big blue eyes and white-blonde hair, who was precious and loved being held and cuddled.

I was thrilled to have my two beautiful and healthy girls. I felt completely fulfilled and loved being a mom to Megan and Allison.

Megan began struggling with self-esteem from an early age. She was taller and bigger-boned than the other kids, which made her a target for bullying. By third grade, Megan was really struggling. She had friends but never felt like she fit in with the popular crowd, who were quick to call her names or exclude her. Megan always thought that if they accepted her, the bullying would stop. She cried a lot at night, and I tried everything to comfort her, but it was clear she needed more help than I could provide.

One night, Megan confided in me that she wanted to kill herself. I was speechless. I didn't know how to respond or what to do. In a panic, I called her pediatrician, who referred us to an adolescent psychologist and psychiatrist. However, getting an appointment was difficult, with waiting lists up to six months. I finally secured an appointment three months out and spent every day until then watching over Megan, hoping the doctor would have a solution.

Megan was diagnosed with depression and ADHD. While medication and therapy helped a little bit, Megan was still struggling with her self-esteem and trying to figure out where she fit in with friend groups. By the end of seventh grade, the bullying was so bad that Megan begged to stay home. She cried every day going to school and coming home from school. I knew we needed to make a change. I enrolled Megan at a new school for her 8th-grade year. Over the summer before the school year started, Megan met some wonderful and supportive friends. She joined the school volleyball team, and by the time school started, Megan was happy and had gained some self-confidence. As a parent, I was so excited to see her smile, laugh with friends, and just be a goofy 13-year-old girl.

In 2006, in the early days of social media, Megan started pestering me about having her own Myspace account before her fourteenth birthday. I was uncomfortable with the idea but eventually agreed under strict supervision. On August 5, 2006, she received a friend request from a boy named Josh Evans. Initially, everything seemed harmless, and Megan was happy.

On October 16, 2006, Megan began receiving a series of mean messages from Josh. It began with, "You heard me. No one likes you; no one wants to be friends with you anymore," and devolved into increasingly personal attacks with other kids joining in. I told her to sign off, but the damage was done. Megan was in tears, feeling utterly devastated.

When I got home and read the messages, I was horrified. I tried to comfort Megan, but she was inconsolable. She ran upstairs, and those were the last words she said to me: "You're supposed to be my mom. You're supposed to be on my side."

I was talking with her dad in the kitchen and then stopped mid-sentence. Pure dread washed over my body. My heart sank, and my whole body felt instantly drained. I knew something was wrong. I can't explain why some parents always know when something is wrong with their children. I bolted upstairs.

I flung open Megan's door and saw she had attempted to take her own life. It's so hard to describe how it feels to experience an event like this. The adrenaline is unbelievable. While the paramedics worked to save her, I had an out-of-body experience. It's like I was there, but just watching everything happen. I had no control; everything was spinning, and my vision was narrowed to a pinpoint with only one thing in focus—Megan. Everything else was static. I just wanted them to say that everything would be okay, that Megan would be fine, and that we didn't need to worry.

After almost 24 hours in the ICU and after the doctors tried everything, Megan's organs were shutting down. We made the choice not to put her on life support. I laid in bed and held her while they took the tubes off her body and turned the machine sounds off. I whispered to her that it was okay to let go and how much I loved her. Her breaths became shallower until there was no more.

When I left the hospital the night Megan died, a part of me died with her. I was no longer the same person. I will never be that person again. Before I lost Megan, I would wake up in the morning with plans and dreams like everyone else. I looked forward to life experiences, vacations, and seeing my girls grow up. All of that was gone in a flash.

I didn't know how to live a life without her. I prayed for God to take me so I could hold her one more time and tell her how much I loved her and that it would be okay. I questioned my ability to be a mom to Allison. I felt if I couldn't save Megan, then what good was I for Allison? The pain was so deep that it hurt to breathe. I needed to have my family and friends around me, but I would so often push them away because I knew my screams, sobs, and deafening silence scared them. Allison was the only one that I wanted to be next to me. I could breathe a little easier for that moment.

We were still navigating the early stages of grief when we learned that the Josh Evans profile was fake. It was created by our neighbor after Megan had a falling out with her daughter. Learning this only intensified my grief, but it was the anger, rage, and vengeance that came to the forefront, demanding justice for Megan. We pressed charges and testified in a federal trial in Los Angeles, California, but ultimately, there was no legal precedent for this type of cyberbullying.

Determined to make a change, I founded the Megan Meier Foundation in 2007 to spread awareness about the devastating effects of bullying and cyberbullying. Our mission was to create a safe and supportive environment for young people and their families. I worked closely with Senator Scott Rupp and Governor Matt Blunt's Internet Task Force for the State of Missouri to help pass Senate Bill 818, which amended harassment and stalking laws to include electronic communication.

The Megan Meier Foundation has become a beacon of hope for countless families affected by bullying, cyberbullying, and suicide. We offer support, education, and advocacy to combat these pervasive issues. What started as a commitment to educating the community about bullying and cyberbullying has grown into so much more. Sixteen years later, the foundation has impacted over 611,000 students, parents, educators, and professionals nationwide through the dedication of staff members, volunteers, family, and friends.

Our programs now include preventative services focusing on mental wellness, connecting youth with information, resources, counseling services, and support. Our goal is to take a proactive approach to mental wellness, addressing issues before they become insurmountable.

The loss of Megan was an unimaginable tragedy that left our family shattered. In the depths of our grief, we found strength in the belief that we could turn our pain into a force for good. The Megan Meier Foundation was born out of this conviction and continues to be a source of hope and support for those in need.

On October 16, 2006, Tina Meier's life changed forever when her 13-year-old daughter, Megan, took her own life after being cyberbullied by a neighbor posing as a fictitious boy on MySpace.

In 2007, Tina founded the Megan Meier Foundation to combat bullying, cyberbullying, and suicide. The foundation has made a significant impact, reaching over 611,000 students, parents, and educators nationwide.

Tina collaborated with Missouri's leaders to pass Senate Bill 818 in 2008. Her advocacy has been featured on various media platforms, including as a TEDx speaker in 2016. She also consulted on the 2011 ABC Family movie Cyberbully. The Megan Meier Foundation has held a certification with the Missouri Department of Mental Health since 2018 and has been a United Way Safety Net member since 2020.

Recognitions include:
- Teen Line's Humanitarian of the Year
- Presidential Invitation to the White House Anti-Bullying Conference
- Judge Arnold Krekel Trailblazer Award
- Women in Leadership honoree
- GRIT Award
- Human Relations Commission Person of the Year 2022

Tina continues to travel nationwide today, inspiring others to "Be Megan's Voice... Be the Change!"

Please scan this QR code to connect with the author.

Paulette Luckett

Choose to Live

Can you imagine a parent being told that they need to get an insurance policy because their child will not live past five years of age? Or being told if you want your child to live, move to Arizona where you know no one and have no support? My mother lived that reality, and I was that child.

Between the ages of 2 and 3, I was diagnosed with asthma. It was scary for my entire family. The asthma was severe and out of control. No one would take me on as a patient besides my pediatrician. One asthma attack could lead to a few hours or a few weeks in the hospital. The ER staff became so familiar with me that when my mother would drop me off at the ER doors as she parked the car, they knew me on sight and would start treating me immediately. Hospitalizations consisted of IVs, oxygen, injections, and blood draws.

One night, the unimaginable happened; the ER was not able to stop/reverse the asthma attack. During normal ER visits, the attack was stopped after 2-3 injections. They had administered 4, and I was on oxygen with no signs of improvement. I was officially in status asthmaticus, known today as acute severe asthma. This is when severe asthma is unresponsive to repeated courses of beta-agonist therapy such as inhaled albuterol, levabuterol, or subcutaneous epinephrine. This is considered a medical emergency that requires immediate diagnosis and treatment. A doctor came in and asked my mother to enter the hallway. I had so much medication in my tiny body that my heart was racing and almost beating out of my chest. I was shaking so hard that the gurney that I was on kept hitting the wall.

My mother was told that since they could not stop the asthma attack, they would need to intubate me. Intubation is a medical procedure where a tube is inserted into a person's mouth or nose and down into their trachea (windpipe). The tube keeps the person's airway open so air can flow into the lungs, helping the person breathe. The tube can open the airway and deliver medication directly into the lungs. She was terrified. While she was in the hallway, I looked up at the ceiling as my body kept shaking. I was so afraid. I still could not catch my breath. I was still wheezing. Then, as I looked up, I saw a bright, warm light. I felt warmth wash over me. I became calm and was no longer afraid. Then I felt a pop on the inside of my chest. Instantly, I could breathe, and I stopped shaking. I sat up on the gurney and then turned so my legs dangled over the edge. I hopped off the gurney, and then, with my IV pole in tow, I walked to the hallway to find my mother.

My mother was down the hall, with her back turned, still speaking with doctors. I walked up, tapped her, and told them I felt better and wanted to go home. She, along with the doctors, looked at me in shock. I was immediately picked up and rushed back into my ER room. They listened to my lungs and heart repeatedly. Each time, they looked confused. They attached an oxygen saturation monitor to determine if I was getting enough oxygen, and I was nearly 100%. Just moments before, my levels were dangerously low, even with oxygen. The doctors met again with my mother out in the hallway. They couldn't explain to my mother why I stopped being short of breath, was no longer wheezing, and my oxygen levels were normal without oxygen. My mother was told we could not leave yet. Their concern is that I may still have been in status asthmaticus. They were afraid and did not want to be held accountable for discharging me if something bad happened. We were there for several more hours. They eventually allowed me to go home. We got home early in the morning, but I went to school the next day. This was unusual. After a severe attack, I would be completely worn out and would sleep much of the next day.

What happened that day? Later in life, I came to believe that I had been visited by an angel and healed. In my opinion, no other explanation answered how and why. I will never forget that night as long as I live.

At my follow-up visit with my pediatrician, Dr. Korn, he informed my mother and me that he had found an allergist named Dr. Herbert Krantman to help me with my asthma. My mother was excited and hopeful, but I had no idea what to think about this news.

Dr. Krantman's office was far from our house. It took forever to get there. We were greeted by Jane, his office manager, and then taken to a room to talk. Dr. Krantman. We talked for quite a while. He then explained how he could help me and what must be done for that to happen. Everything was going well until he explained the allergy test. When he mentioned tiny needles in the skin of my back, having allergic reactions, and the possibility that it could be severe. I became afraid and asked to leave. Honestly, I panicked. And started crying. He gave my mother and me a few minutes. Once I calmed down, he came back. He asked my mother if it was okay if he and I talked alone. My mother gave her permission and left the room.

The conversation that we had was one of the most important ones of my life at that time. Dr. Krantman acknowledged my fears being valid with all the trauma I endured from the severe asthma attacks, hospital visits, hospitalizations, and all of the needles I had been stuck with. What he said next was monumental. He said, "Paulette, you will have to decide today that you want to live." Imagine how that sounded to someone 7 or 8 years of age. He explained that only I could make the decision about going through the allergy testing and starting weekly allergy shots. He promised that my symptoms would get better, I would gain better control of my asthma, and I would have fewer asthma attacks. But this was all on the other side of allergy testing. We talked longer, and I agreed to have the allergy testing done. I was still afraid of the needles, but I wanted a better life where asthma didn't dictate/control my life. I wanted a life. I wanted to live. The allergy testing was not as bad as I thought, but the itching and reactions were terrible. I was allergic to almost everything they tested me for except foods. My specific allergy shot formulation could now be mixed, and I would start the following week.

Going to Dr. Krantman's office weekly was a huge change that came with challenges. I am so thankful for my grandparents, who helped make getting there easier. As promised, after some time, my symptoms improved, my asthma became manageable, my medications worked as they should, and I had fewer asthma attacks. My visits became easier. Two shots, one in each arm then a 15-minute wait in the waiting room to make sure I did not have a reaction. I took allergy shots for almost two years. I never experienced an adverse reaction.

That decision to go forward with allergy testing and then allergy shots changed my life and allowed me to finally start to live. Before, everything was restricted. I could not play outside. I could not go to anyone's house that wasn't family due to the severity of my asthma diagnosis and my mother's fear. My mother did not sleep well for years. My asthma was nocturnal, and the symptoms showed up at night. I could be in a deep sleep and be having a full asthma attack. I remember feeling my mother's hand on my back and/or chest, checking my breathing.

Again, I started to live… I am sure you are wondering what that looked like. I started to go outside and play, ride my bike, and roam my grandparent's neighborhood instead of being restricted to my grandparent's yard, participate in gym class without fear, and take swimming lessons. I then ran Summer track. It was challenging the first year. Due to my diagnosis, I participated in the walk race. I then started long-distance running. The following year, something changed, and it just did not work. They changed me to sprinting, which was exactly what I needed. The entire season, I would start to have an asthma attack after every race. My mother or coach would be at the finish line waiting with my inhaler. It got better. Can you imagine the use to be out of control asthmatic running the first or fourth leg of a relay? I did it!

What else did I do? I ran on the high school track team and became the first Black drum major at Ladue Horton Watkins Senior High School during my Junior and senior years. It was all because I chose to live.

I know that life can throw some serious curveballs and blows, but you have to decide that you don't want to survive but want to live. As women, we go through so much in our bodies, minds, families, and personal relationships. These things should not dictate your life! Only God and you can!

Don't let what your mother or father said, what the doctor said, or what your significant other said dictate whether you live, survive, or die. Hunni, you were created to live well. Do It!

Surviving is not an option; only living….

Paulette Luckett is a Registered Nurse, child health advocate, and podcast hostess.

She is a proud school nurse for a middle school in the St. Louis Public Schools district in the City of St. Louis.

In March of 2024, she became the first school nurse in her district to obtain a certification from the National Board for Certification of School Nurses (NBSCN), making her a nationally certified school nurse.

In August 2023, she released the first episode of her podcast, "The School Nurse Chronicles." This podcast was started to bridge the gap between the school nurse's office, the school, and the community by sharing real-life issues happening in schools that affect students' physical, mental, and emotional health.

Paulette wants to grow her listeners and followers so that students, staff, and parents can become empowered and informed and make better decisions for their students.

Soon, she will host Hot Topic in-person Meet-Ups.

Please scan this QR code to connect with the author.

Porscha Anderson

Unveiling Purpose:
A Journey of Resilience and Discovery

Finding purpose is a deeply personal and transformative journey, often beginning in the most unexpected places. My journey to discovering my purpose started in the 4th grade with a remarkable teacher named Mrs. Elizabeth Smith. She was an incredible woman—beautiful, intelligent, and deeply compassionate. Mrs. Smith saw something in me—a spark of potential that I hadn't yet recognized in myself. One day, she received permission from my mother to take me to church with her. Mrs. Smith oversaw the children's choir and played the piano. In that sacred space, surrounded by hymns and melodies, I remember meeting God for the first time.

By middle school, Mrs. Smith and I had lost touch, but the seeds of faith and purpose she planted within me continued to grow. Reflecting on this time in my life, I realize how significantly our childhood shapes who we are, our belief systems, and our pursuit of purpose. The experiences and influences we encounter as children lay the groundwork for our values, aspirations, and understanding of the world.

The people we look up to in our formative years play a crucial role in shaping our beliefs and aspirations. Mrs. Smith was a beacon of compassion, intelligence, and faith. Her belief in me helped build my self-confidence and showed me the power of having someone believe in me. Her influence made me aspire to be a teacher. I was inspired by her example and the powerful Black women educators who embodied a no-nonsense approach to life and loved what they did.

The Power of Resilience

Even as a young girl, I felt a calling to change the world significantly. The path wasn't always clear, but the desire to make a difference was unwavering. I wanted to be a teacher, inspired by the powerful examples of Black women in my life who were not only smart and educated but also embodied a no-nonsense approach to life and loved what they did. Their influence and strength left an indelible mark on me, shaping my vision for my future and igniting a passion for purpose-driven living.

Then, during my sophomore year in high school, I got pregnant. I was embarrassed and ashamed. I was very disappointed in myself because I knew I was meant for more. I felt like I had let myself and my family down. I remember thinking, how will you be great in life and fulfill this big purpose as a teenage mother? I contemplated abortion, but I knew that I wasn't ready for the consequences or karma that would come with that. I went through a long period of denial. Eventually, I decided to take ownership of my choice and have the baby. I hid my pregnancy from my family for seven months. I had held out for as long as I could before I told my mom. When I finally told her, I could sense the disappointment, but she took it better than I thought. After having my son, my purpose shifted to being a great mother and provider.

Discovering a New Path

I graduated high school, enrolled in college, and began working to become a better version of myself to be an example for my child. Although I couldn't see it then, my purpose was all around me. My lived experience as a mother shaped the type of person, teacher, and leader I would become. It taught me resilience, determination, and the importance of setting a positive example.

In my late twenties, I finally had a sense of purpose. I realized that purpose was pursuing me all along. It was always there; I had to be still and let it find me. At the age of 27, I started my first business. I always loved fashion and making people look and feel their best. That brought me so much joy. That evolved into helping people with their business and finances. Since then, I have had great successes and failures in business that have shaped who I am today. These experiences have developed resilience and an evolving sense of purpose.

Purpose in Action

Through my journey, I found my calling as a certified life and business coach, specifically helping women over 40 activate their purpose and achieve their dreams. This role embodies my purpose in action. It allows me to use my skills, experiences, and passion to make a meaningful impact on the lives of others.

I help women recognize their potential, set and achieve their goals, and navigate their challenges. Many of the women I work with are still searching for their purpose. They have unfulfilled dreams and desires that have haunted them, leading to a life of regret and disappointment. My mission is to guide them through self-discovery, helping them identify their strengths, passions, and values. Together, we create actionable plans to achieve their dreams and live fulfilling lives.

Seeing these women transform, regain their confidence, and pursue their passions with renewed vigor reaffirms that my purpose is to help others find and fulfill their own.

Purpose Will Find You

Purpose will find you. It will present itself as opportunities, often in ways you least expect. Sometimes, we believe that purpose must be grand and visible, putting us in the spotlight where others can see our achievements. We imagine purpose as a destination, a pinnacle of success where everything falls into place. However, this perception can be misleading.

Purpose is not always about public recognition or accolades. It is often found in the quiet moments when we act with intention and compassion. It is in the small, consistent actions we take to improve ourselves and help those around us. Purpose reveals itself in the opportunities to make a difference, whether big or small, and in how we respond to the challenges and blessings that come our way.

Your Purpose is Already in You

Your purpose is already in you. It is woven into the fabric of your being, shaped by your experiences, passions, and values. Sometimes, it takes time and self-reflection to uncover, but it is always there, waiting to be realized. Purpose is not a fixed destination but a journey that evolves as you grow and change.

As you navigate through life, your understanding of your purpose may shift. What drives you today might differ from what motivates you tomorrow, and that's perfectly okay. Allow yourself the freedom to explore different paths and embrace new possibilities. Your purpose can adapt to the changing seasons of your life, reflecting your growth and the lessons you learn along the way.

What Does Walking in Purpose Look Like?

Walking on purpose looks like living authentically and intentionally. It means aligning your actions with your values and passions, even when challenging. It's about making choices that resonate with your true self and contribute to the greater good.

Walking on purpose involves:

- **Resilience**: Facing obstacles with determination and viewing setbacks as opportunities for growth. It's about bouncing back stronger and more focused on your goals.

- **Compassion**: Acting with kindness and empathy toward yourself and others. It's about understanding the impact you can have and choosing to uplift and support those around you.

- **Dedication**: Committing to your passions and goals with unwavering dedication. It's about putting in the effort and staying persistent, even when the path is difficult.

- **Authenticity**: Being true to yourself, embracing your unique qualities, and not conforming to others' expectations. It's about honoring your truth and living in a way that reflects your deepest values.

Walking on purpose is a dynamic process. It's not about having everything figured out but about continuously striving to live a life that feels meaningful and fulfilling.

Reimagining Purpose

I encourage you to reimagine purpose. Don't confine it to a single definition or a specific path. Purpose is multifaceted and can be found in various aspects of your life. It's in your relationships, work, hobbies, and dreams. It's in the way you connect with others, the impact you have, and the legacy you leave behind.

Reimagine purpose as something fluid and expansive. Allow it to grow with you, to be shaped by your experiences and the people you meet. Embrace the idea that your purpose may change over time and that each phase of your life can bring new and fulfilling opportunities.

Think of purpose as a journey, not a destination. It's about the process of becoming, continuously evolving, and finding new ways to live meaningfully. It's about being open to the unexpected and finding joy in the present moment.

In reimagining your purpose, give yourself the grace to explore, make mistakes, and learn. Trust that you are on the right path, even when it doesn't look like you imagined. Your purpose is unique to you and will unfold in its own time and way.

Finding your purpose is a deeply personal and often complex journey. It requires patience, resilience, and an open heart. Embrace your unique path, stay true to your passions, seek guidance, and practice perseverance.

Your purpose is in you, waiting to be discovered. Embrace the journey, trust in the process, and let your purpose unfold in its own beautiful and unique way. Your journey is yours alone, and it holds the power to inspire and transform not only your life but the lives of those around you.

Porscha Anderson is an award-winning business strategist and life and performance coach who empowers women over 40 to realize their fullest potential.

She is the Founder of PLA Enterprise, a distinguished coaching and consulting firm dedicated to facilitating personal and professional growth. With an extensive background as an entrepreneur, international speaker, and author of "The Art of Unleashing Your Inner R.E.B.E.L.," Porscha's journey towards authenticity began with a profound personal awakening that compelled her to redefine her beliefs and uncover her true self.

Leveraging her transformative experiences, she adeptly guides clients through unlearning limiting beliefs, redefining their narratives, and manifesting their deepest aspirations. Porscha's empathetic and insightful coaching methodology empowers women to transcend societal constraints and lead lives marked by boldness and integrity.

Her work epitomizes the strength found in vulnerability, courage, and relentless self-discovery. Based in St. Louis, MO, Porscha continues to inspire and mentor women globally, guiding them toward lives enriched with purpose, authenticity, and limitless potential.

Please scan this QR code to connect with the author.

Vickie Calmese

From Tears to Triumph! What a Journey!

It was May 1966, and Rock Jr. High School in East St. Louis, IL, was bustling with activity, excitement, and anticipation for the annual event commemorating academic achievements. The school gymnasium was adorned with purple and gold colors, and an awards table was decorated with candles. No, it wasn't a regular graduation, but it was very special. It was a well-attended, beautiful, sacred, and memorable ceremony. A small for her age, an 11-year-old black girl fashionably wearing a yellow dress with ruffles, matching yellow shoes, and hair pulled back in a ponytail tied with a yellow bow and bangs, walked across the stage to much applause. She had just been inducted into the prestigious National Junior Honor Society, which required applicants to demonstrate excellence in leadership, citizenship, character, service, and scholarship.

On that warm spring day, she walked home from the ceremony alone—no family, no friends. The tears she shed stained her certificate and blurred out her name. I am THAT GIRL! A life-changing decision was made during that walk—that I would always be present, especially for my children!

My mother was away "singing on the road." She had a beautiful alto voice. My mother, aunt, and maternal grandmother sang in a local gospel group and recorded several Gospel albums. At some point in her singing career, she also sang background for Lionel Richie and the Commodores. Lionel Richie sent a telegram of condolences for my mother's funeral. Singing and music was a major part of my life. My younger sister followed in the musical footsteps of our mother. As a single mother with three daughters, she provided well for us. We never lacked any material possessions. We never went hungry or had our utilities cut off. We didn't own a car, but we had access to over 100 taxi cabs, as our mother also worked as a cab dispatcher when she wasn't on the road. It was like we had 100 private chauffeurs that we referred to as "uncles." To avoid being totally dependent on them, we had to learn to ride the city bus. It took a village to raise us, and we had a great village.

That day conjured up feelings not of anger but of hurt, despair, and loneliness. You may have heard the familiar saying, "Spare the rod, spoil the child." Suffice it to say I was not spoiled. Not getting or having your way as a pre-teen seemed like the normal way of life...a life of despair. As a middle child, loneliness was never an issue. The culturally accepted and expected norms of the early 1960s had three generations of family geographically close. Momma, Grandma/Mudear, and Big Momma lived either with you, upstairs, next door, or right down the street. Loneliness, however, was a new, unknown feeling. This cultural phenomenon was so embedded in my behavior that even after marriage, I ended up living down the street from my mother/grandmother and around the corner from my sister.

The significance and impact of that day set me on a path of self-appreciation! I had learned you couldn't always rely on others to show up for you. Those tears watered the seeds of caring expressed through the gift of presence. So began my journey from tears to triumph!

Growing up in a socio-economically deprived area yielded limited resources in all areas of life. Formalized recreation activities were pretty much non-existent. Mostly, we went outside and played, although I did learn to roller skate in the All-Purpose room of my elementary school. Attending church activities was not an option; it was a requirement for living in my mother's house. School was considered our "job"; therefore, I wanted to be a "good worker." I focused on church, school, and play in that order. That was it. Our clothes were even designated by those three activities. We had church clothes, school clothes, and play clothes.

I soon began to see the value of school and academic success as "killing two birds with one stone." I could please my mother and get off of the hamster wheel of impoverished living I witnessed on a daily basis. I became a great student and an avid reader. Reading served as an escape to other places, meeting different people, and experiencing lifestyles foreign to my way of life. Humor served as a survival tool to offset some of the dysfunction I became accustomed to in my community. Setting the priorities of Christ, curiosity, and courage now became the fuel and energy that provided the necessary motivation to navigate through my life's journey.

Tears were plentiful from getting "whoopings," which hurt me then but taught me discipline, respect, obedience, and the knowledge that behavior has consequences. I soon learned all "whoopings" aren't physical either. The impact of emotional "whoopings" lasts a lot longer than the pain from a physical one. *(I'll take physical whoopings for $500, Alex, LOL.)* Bad decisions, youthful mistakes, and hanging with the wrong crowds all caused many tears for me, as well as my mother. I was a great student and a mischievous child. Nobody's perfect.

The triumph of my early childhood discipline helped me:

- Develop a relationship with GOD. Who else could I "tell all my troubles to? All of that mandatory church attendance, Sunday school, vacation bible school, mid-week prayer service, and singing in the choir provided me with a solid relationship with Christ and numerous social skills. I smiled when I didn't want to, spoke to people/teachers I didn't know, and actively listened to others.

- Excel academically, which allowed me to be awarded "straight A student" ticket vouchers to attend Cardinal baseball games. Getting out of town and sitting in Busch Stadium gave me such a thrill that I got straight A's for almost six years.

- Believe in myself and accept that I can be different even if I am not accepted. I didn't believe in conformity if it made no sense to me. Maybe I was rebellious. I believe my constant reading opened my mind to a variety of solutions and possibilities for living.

Then I entered teenage hood, ages 14-15, and "courting." There were tears of heartbreak from puppy love, which can be a devastating time in any young girl's life. I was no exception to that rule. Again, I relied upon my priorities and prayed to God. I didn't want to have to kiss too many frogs to find my prince. My curiosity gave me the courage to keep kissing. Miraculously, I only had three boyfriends before I found my prince. The triumph is that my prince, now my king, and I will celebrate 50 years of marriage on June 29, 2024, even before this chapter is in print.

Ironically, my husband is a minister, even though he wasn't when we got married. He eventually became a pastor for 31 years. Maybe all that mandatory church attendance predisposed me to marry a preacher. Who knew?

We have two children. Our daughter was born first *(the way it should be, LOL)*, and five years later, our son was born. The decision and vow I made to myself as an 11-year-old girl was being manifested. I attended every piano recital, musical instrument concert, spoken word recital, stage play, karate competition, and singing concert they participated in. Some of those events brought tears to my eyes, tears of sorrow, laughter, and joy. Sometimes, the sorrow was because the concert sounded so bad, laughter because some of the events were just funny, and joy when I would see their faces light up with smiles as they looked for me and spotted me in the crowd.

Oh, for the tears shed during childbirth, there are no words. However, the triumph of being present for our children has allowed us to have memorable experiences. We have some amazing children! Being present for them has meant going on our first Disney cruise in 2004 to the Eastern Caribbean islands of St. Thomas, St. Croix, St. Maarten, and the Bahamas, where our son played the part of Simba in The Lion King as an independent contractor. Thanks to our daughter, we were present at the birth of our only grandchild in 2007. Being present also started a mother-daughter bonding tradition via annual attendance at the Muny and The Fabulous Fox Theater, which has lasted over 16 years. We were present in Beijing, China, and Taiwan in 2009 and 2012 as our son played Mereb in the classic play AIDA. In 2015, we were present as our daughter received an award for "30 Leaders in their 30's," sponsored by North County Incorporated.

The gift of presence cannot be underestimated. It has enriched my life and the lives of those who receive it. Time is the foundation of presence. When we receive presence, it comes from the irreplaceable conduit of time. The tears of a little black girl from East St. Louis, IL, have yielded a plethora of triumphs just by being present.

Vickie Calmese is a daughter, wife, and mother. She grew up in the "great 89 Blocks," also known as East St. Louis, IL, and resides in St. Louis, MO.

For the past 50 years, Vickie has been a devoted wife. She and her husband reared two children. She has also served as a church's "First Lady" for 31 years.

In 1986, she started her first business, Calmese Creations, showcasing her self-taught skills as a seamstress. A registered nurse since 1974, she ventured into the healthcare industry in 1999 with IMPACT Managed Care, a case management company focused on workers' comp rehabilitation clients.

She created HEALTHLARIOUS in 2013, which provides healthcare education in a standup comedic format. This business continues to give her the most joy.

Vickie is an integral part of Morning Glory Nation, an international online ministry that connects people to Christ and each other. The group's daily 6:30 a.m. live streams feature biblical teachings, prayers, and empowerment strategies. Sometimes called "Mama Vickie," she facilitates the ministry's "Mind, Body, and Spirit" segment, regularly hosting experts on health and wellness.

Please scan this QR code to connect with the author.

Kim Fletcher

My Story Isn't Over Yet

I almost died. It was Friday, January 11, 2013—a day forever etched in my memory.

When I donned my stylish skirt and sweater that morning, a stroke was the furthest thing from my mind. I admit, though, I feared the possibility. Maybe not that day. But one day.

My worry wasn't a nagging, everyday fear. It was more subconscious—a hidden anxiety that lay dormant until I woke up with a headache or random pain. Then fear reared its ugly head. The symptoms were usually false alarms, but the internal panic often lingered long after doctors confirmed that everything was okay.

I'm no hypochondriac. My fears were warranted. My mom died at 55 from a massive heart attack brought on by a string of health issues. I pulled the lucky genetic straw and received a similar diagnosis at 12 years old. Hospital visits, medical exams, and blood pressure medicines were staples in my otherwise wonderful childhood.

So were seeds of fear.

Doctors painted a bleak picture of my adult years based on my test results. Despite my healthy lifestyle, I had a predisposition for serious health complications, a fact that took up silent residence in my psyche. Plus, I watched my mother battle valiantly, only to have her life cut short just two years after my dad's early departure. I wondered if my fate would be the same.

But not this day. I zipped down the highway without a care on that crisp January morning. An hour later, after an uplifting Bible study, I walked outside with my friend and mentor, who led the gathering. I don't recall our exact conversation, but I'm sure we rejoiced over God's goodness. No matter where our talks started, they always seemed to end up there.

This time was no different…until it *was* different.

I suddenly felt a wobbliness in my feet as we chatted. At first, I didn't pay much attention to the odd sensation, but the tremors quickly traveled up my entire body. And that's how it all began—a whirlwind of prayer, calls to 911, blaring sirens, and flights carrying my siblings. I suffered a hemorrhagic stroke, or in my doctor's layman's terms, "it's when a blood vessel in the brain bursts, like a leaky pipe."

Doctors were upfront with my brothers and sister, letting them know there was nothing they could do. Like everyone else, they simply waited to see if the bleeding would stop. According to my family, they weren't optimistic. My brother Jeff, a long-time military serviceman who witnessed many emergency scenes, recalled how the staff's body language signaled their doubt that I would survive.

These same doctors were off duty that weekend but returned to work Monday morning. Jeff saw them walking down the hall. He said their eyes widened when they glanced through my room window. They were shocked to see me alive.

The days, weeks, and months that followed were hard. I experienced emotional distress and displayed attitudes and behaviors that I'm not proud of. During one of my lowest points, a question tormented me throughout the night: "Is Jesus even real?" Another Bible study teacher and her husband offered to let me stay with them while I completed six months of physical therapy. She came into my room the following day and immediately sensed my anxiety. After I spilled my doubts, she gave me advice that seemed unhelpful at the time but, in hindsight, was just what I needed to hear.

"You need to read the Bible," she said, "particularly the New Testament. Don't skip around, don't stop to look up words, and even if it seems like a fairytale, keep reading. When you get to the end, read it again." I've been reading the Bible like this for eleven years now. God's word has anchored me through some of my toughest times and brought me to a place of genuine joy and hope.

Fast forward to January 2023, almost ten years to the day of my stroke. I cleaned out a file cabinet in my home office and found a folder with my medical records and the cards that had poured in. One of my siblings must have tucked the file away while I was in the hospital. I had never seen it before. As I sat on the floor and read every word, a friend's annual challenge came to mind. We each picked a "word of the year" as our guiding principle to carry us through the months that awaited us. My word crystallized at that moment.

Onward.

As soon as it pierced my thoughts, I knew it was time. It was time to let go of the lingering emotional effects that still held parts of me captive. I got up, gathered the papers and cards, and threw them in the trash… grateful for where God had brought me and excited about the road ahead.

**

Although our stories are different, one thing is true for all of us: we will encounter hard times. Some troubles are minor irritations. Others are mountains that seem impossible to get around. That's how I felt after my stroke. But as I look back, what felt like the end was the start of a new beginning. I leave you with a few life lessons that continue to guide and ground me today. May they do the same for you.

Run to God in troubles, not away from him. My faith means everything to me, and that's not an exaggeration. So, I didn't know how to respond when I began to question the existence of the one I'd dedicated my life to, the Lord Jesus Christ. I am so grateful that my Bible study teacher implored me to "read the Bible." Her simple advice brought hope and healing.

I encourage you to remain faithful to God in difficult times. He can carry you through the most horrific circumstances. The process may not be easy and may not happen overnight, but when you run to him, his words will ring true:

"Come to me, all of you who are weary and burdened, and I will give you rest. Take my yoke upon you and learn from me, because I am lowly and humble in heart, and you will find rest for your souls" (Matthew 11:28-29, CSB).

Face your fears. Fear can make us do illogical and, frankly, stupid things. I likely could have prevented my stroke by monitoring my blood pressure more closely. Instead, I chose to ignore reality. But the facts stared me in the face after I woke up in the hospital. I had to take better care of myself, and more importantly, address the fear that had dogged me most of my life. Nothing changed at that moment, but over time, I unpacked years of wrong mindsets about my health. Today, I enjoy a freedom that I never knew was possible.

Extreme fear is not our friend, so let's eliminate it from our lives, no matter how difficult the process may be. Our freedom is worth the effort.

Get rid of guilt. Guilt burdened me for many years. I constantly replayed, "This is all my fault. I wouldn't be in this situation if I'd only done a few small things." It's normal to regret decisions that harm ourselves or others, but wallowing in guilt won't change the past. Let us accept God's forgiveness and commit to better decisions and behaviors from this day forward. Even if people choose not to forgive us, we must forgive ourselves.

Lean on your support system. I have amazing family and friends. I've kept much of the same routine because of their generosity and support. I often tell people, "There's no way I could have stayed in St. Louis—without family and without driving—were it not for my selfless, gracious, patient friends." Their love reminds me of a well-known Bible verse: *"...a real friend sticks closer than a brother"* (Proverbs 18:24, NLT).

Whether you're in a peaceful place or a challenging one, never take for granted those who stick with you through thick and thin. They are priceless. That may be one person; it may be more. The number is not as important as the intent: to keep you moving forward and to bring out your best. True friends are a treasure. Be sure to let them know.

Know your true identity. I remember the day I sat in my wheelchair in the back of the medical bus, watching the trees whiz by. "How did I end up here?" I thought. I had gone from business executive to patient, from sitting in an office chair to sitting in a wheelchair, from the lady with a five-year career plan to the woman who struggled to plan for the next hour. That day marked the first step toward discovering my true identity. Honestly, I thought I already had this figured out. Yet, when the titles and career accolades meant nothing, I realized how much I still depended on them.

Our careers, our circumstances, and people's opinions don't define us. They are temporary and can change in the blink of an eye. What matters is the character we display when no one is watching and how we treat others. Let's strive to do both well.

Remember, this is *your* journey. I needed time to return to a stable mental and emotional state...a lot of time. I've experienced other hardships and always seemed to recover at a "reasonable" pace. But this trauma hit differently. I no longer felt like myself. Not just physically but emotionally too. I wasn't motivated, I battled depression, and I got lazy. It took me years to turn the corner.

Now that I'm in a much better space, I realize we can't be moved by other people's expectations of how quickly we should heal. No one can tell you when or how you should handle tough times, and you shouldn't feel obligated to follow their formula. This is not to say that people you trust can't offer sound guidance, but at the end of the day, this journey is your own. Your bounce back may happen in short order, or it may take time. That's okay. Time isn't the best gauge of victory; you are.

Keep going...your story isn't over. "My story isn't over yet" has become my favorite phrase in recent years. It's my way to sum up my survival, God's faithfulness, and my excitement about what's ahead. I can't predict the future. More challenges may lurk around the corner. I've learned, though, that no matter how big the obstacle, I can make it.

So, no, my story isn't over yet.

And neither is yours.

Kim Fletcher has loved stories for as long as she can remember. Her fondest childhood memories center around much-anticipated library visits with her mom and settling into the family's yellow bean bag chair to enjoy her next literary adventure.

That passion fueled her decision to major in journalism at Florida A&M University. After college, Kim managed the daily company newsletter at Hallmark Cards in Kansas City, Missouri. She later moved to St. Louis and began a 15-year career at one of the world's leading public relations agencies.

After nearly 20 years in the corporate sector, Kim decided to pursue her dream of book publishing. Today, she provides editing services to new and aspiring authors. In her spare time, she enjoys mentoring, participating in Bible studies, and getting lost in a good page-turner.

Please scan this QR code to connect with the author.

Tamara Keefe

Clementine's: Serving Success One Scoop At A Time

One beautiful spring morning, as I shared coffee with friends on the dock overlooking the glistening Lake of the Ozarks, a simple question about how I was doing caused me to break down completely. I had organized this girl's weekend, desperately craving their company. "We have to do a girl's weekend, and soon!" I had emphatically told my friends. They started to believe I was going to announce a dire health diagnosis. Instead, it was a mental health crisis that had taken hold of me, and their inquiry brought it all to the surface.

Outwardly, I seemed to have it all in corporate America, but I was utterly miserable. I had hoped this weekend would be therapeutic, a chance to connect with my friends, and it certainly was. I unleashed all my emotions about my current life. As a high-level senior executive for a major consumer packaged goods company, I spent most of my life on airplanes, traveling 262 days out of the year. Despite a fabulous salary, I had no time for a personal life—no partner, no family involvement, and rarely even time for friends. I was absolutely miserable and broke down sobbing with my girlfriends. Sometimes, the American dream of a huge corporate job is not the heavenly outcome we hope for. One of my friends bluntly told me, "You need to quit!" I was shocked. Another friend said,

"Why don't you go back to making ice cream? Ice cream is what gives you joy. You are always complaining St. Louis does not have good ice cream, and our neighborhood doesn't have a parlor." Both of these suggestions stopped me in my tracks.

I have been making ice cream my whole life. When I was a child, ice cream entirely changed my sense of community and my sense of self. We grew up below the poverty line, and after church on Sundays, the other families in our community would meet at the local ice cream parlor. I remember tugging on my mom's dress, begging her for us to join them, unaware of the financial burden a trip to the ice cream parlor would cause our family of seven. I can still feel the sting of loneliness from being unable to join the rest of our community.

Then, one day, we stopped at a garage sale (that's where we got our clothes), and my mom ran across an old hand-crank ice cream maker for $2 and decided it was going home with us. That was the day my life changed forever. As a family, we made ice cream together, and the sweetest tradition was born. Word of our amazing creations spread, and soon enough, rather than going out for ice cream, the church families began to gather at our house, with each family bringing a different ingredient. I went from social zero to hero! My whole sense of community changed because of ice cream. Suddenly, I had friends, invitations to parties, and a sense of belonging I'd never known before. I became popular and discovered ice cream's power without even realizing it.

Back to that day at the dock, when I broke down, I realized that ice cream was about to change my life a second time. That weekend, my three friends and I wrote my business and marketing plan, put together my financials, and I resigned two weeks later. What was the worst thing that could happen? Yes, I could fail, but I was highly employable and could go back. I had nothing to lose except my pride and money. I cut ties with my high-powered corporate job and was about to become an entrepreneur. In early 2014, I attended "Ice Cream College" at Penn State. I was on the road to happiness.

I didn't set out to create something new in the market. I set out to create something better.

At first, I produced ice cream and sold it through private parties. I offered the hostess free ice cream and asked to have a sign-up sheet available to allow guests to order pints of ice cream delivered to their homes by me. This was before any door delivery services existed, and I was the delivery person. I sold ice cream to hip, cool, and influential restaurants where I knew they would put me on their menus, getting branding on their menus. I knew branding, and I learned how to engage the press. I developed a following and opened Clementine's Naughty and Nice Creamery in Lafayette Square in Saint Louis in 2015.

For the next several years, it was all about making it and owning my destiny. I took no paycheck for the first three years. I am completely self-funded and solely owned by me. I've invested almost $500,000 from my savings, cashed out my 401k, and continue to grow from profits. Having grown up in poverty, I was always in survival mode. As an adult, I was constantly looking for control and stability.

Then, at about the time we opened our third store, my focus began to shift. It went from being about me to being about my team and what we were building here in St. Louis. I became aware of the families depending on the business and our city. I fell in love with St. Louis when I first moved here for a corporate job in 2008, and I have a powerful and never-ending love for this city. St. Louis is an accessible city with affordable housing, free museums, and a booming sense of community, something I had not experienced in other cities around the country. There is something for everyone in this city, and I am proud to call St. Louis home.

What motivated me changed; it felt like an organic evolution. We were innovating in a space where there had been none since Dippin Dots in the 60's and 70's. We were the first to introduce and develop a trade secret process for boozy ice cream, and we began to include products for everyone, including ice cream for vegan and lactose intolerant persons. Suddenly, it was no longer just about me 'making it' but more about the impact on my community of patrons, my teams working in the company, and a thriving St. Louis.

As my company looks to capitalize on our momentum and take advantage of the market opportunity, we will be considering smart outside investments that can help take us to the next level in becoming a national brand. As part of that strategy, we needed to increase our production capacity. Now, we have our offices and new production facility in the poorest zip code in St. Louis, paying living-wage jobs to our employees. I feel strongly that the business owners of St. Louis need to lead the way in alleviating poverty and lifting people.

The city of St. Louis is my true love, and making ice cream is more than a passion; it is also a way to build community and impact lives. I thank my friends for that day on the dock at Lake of the Ozarks, where my epiphany and my utter vulnerability led to new challenges, opportunities, and a happy life in a city I love.

Tamara Keefe, founder of St. Louis-based Clementine's Naughty and Nice Creamery, has always had a deep passion for ice cream and what it represents: family, community, and, in her words, "moments of connection."

Her life's journey from a girl born into an economically disadvantaged family—growing up on food stamps—to a self-made ice cream entrepreneur is nothing short of extraordinary.

Keefe has over 25 years of experience working across global brands in the consumer packaged goods industry. She has worked in multiple functions, focusing on strategy, brand management, consumer insights, and innovation.

A graduate and alum of the Goldman Sachs 10KSB program, as well as a Tory Burch 2019 Foundation Fellow and James Beard 2020 Women's Entrepreneurial Leadership Fellow, Keefe also serves on the board of the St. Louis Civic Pride Foundation.

She is an active member of the Entrepreneurs Organization (EO) and currently serves as MyEO Chair (2019, 2020, 2021), helping businesses grow and thrive.

Please scan this QR code to connect with the author.

Made in the USA
Monee, IL
19 April 2025

15942891R00085